Traditional Projects

Traditional Projects

The Editors of
Fine Woodworking

The Taunton Press

The Taunton Press
Inspiration for hands-on living®

The Taunton Press, Inc., 63 South Main Street, PO Box 5506, Newtown, CT 06470-5506
e-mail: tp@taunton.com

Jacket/Cover design: Susan Fazekas
Interior design and layout: Sue Mattero
Front cover photographer: Michael Pekovich, courtesy *Fine Woodworking*,
© The Taunton Press, Inc.
Back cover photographers: (left) Matt Berger, courtesy *Fine Woodworking*, © The Taunton Press, Inc.;
(right top & bottom) Michael Pekovich, courtesy *Fine Woodworking*, © The Taunton Press, Inc.

The New Best of Fine Woodworking® is a trademark of The Taunton Press, Inc.,
registered in the U.S. Patent and Trademark Office.

Library of Congress Cataloging-in-Publication Data
Traditional projects / The editors of Fine woodworking.
     p. cm. -- (The new best of fine woodworking)
  ISBN 1-56158-784-2
  1. Furniture making--Amateurs' manuals. I. Fine woodworking. II. Series.
  TT195.T7 2005
  684.1'04--dc22

                           2005005400

Printed in the United States of America
10 9 8 7 6 5 4 3 2 1

The following manufacturers/names appearing in *Traditional Projects* are trademarks: Bendheim[SM], Kiwi®,
KlockitSM, McCloskey®, Minwax®, Olde Century Colors®, X-Acto®, Waterlox®

Working with wood is inherently dangerous. Using hand or power tools improperly or ignoring safety practices can lead to permanent injury or even death. Don't try to perform operations you learn about here (or elsewhere) unless you're certain they are safe for you. If something about an operation doesn't feel right, don't do it. Look for another way. We want you to enjoy the craft, so please keep safety foremost in your mind whenever you're in the shop.

Acknowledgments

Special thanks to the authors, editors, art directors, copy editors, and other staff members of *Fine Woodworking* who contributed to the development of the articles in this book.

Contents

Introduction

When I was new to woodworking, I was determined to build pieces only of my own design. One of my design tenets was that a piece of furniture gained something from the use of multiple species of wood, the more the better. It was during this early period that I conceived a tall, straight-backed chair of walnut, ash, and oak inspired by the ergonomics of a skyscraper. Besides being uncoordinated visually, the chair lacked the essential function of comfort. I had spent 40 hours making the equivalent of a stump. Later that winter I chainsawed the chair into small pieces and tossed them into the fireplace. I finally had succeeded in coaxing a few minutes of comfort from my first chair.

That failed project taught me that I had a lot to learn from the masters. I went back to work building classic pieces in the Shaker and Craftsman traditions, which fit in well with my home. But more importantly, they were functional, too.

Whether you aspire to design your own work or simply need plans to walk you through the process of building useful pieces, the projects in this collection provide a great variety of challenges and styles to suit many skill levels and tastes.

Tables large and small are included, as are beds designed in high style or with storage in mind. Need more storage? Build a blanket chest or a chest of drawers. Want

something smaller? Try your hand at building a wall-hung corner cabinet.

Culled from the pages of *Fine Woodworking* magazine, these projects walk you through the process of building and finishing elegant works of furniture that have stood the test of time. If you decide to design your own furniture some day, the skills you learn building these traditional pieces will help you avoid using a chainsaw to undo mistakes.

—Anatole Burkin, Editor
Fine Woodworking

Harvest Table

BY CHRISTIAN
BECKSVOORT

**THIS SHAKER DROP-LEAF
DESIGN can be built for two
or for twenty.**

The drop-leaf table is one of the most versatile designs that I build. I've made small, 30-in.-square end tables, 10-footers for major dinner parties, tables with drawers, tables with one leaf, and tables with leaves that hang almost to the floor. The form can be used not just for dining tables but also for side, end, serving, and couch tables.

Recently, I was commissioned to design and construct a drop-leaf table and a set of chairs to seat eight. The base should provide diners with adequate chair space, with no one straddling a leg. Figuring 24 in. (or more) per serving area, I came up with a base that's 28½ in. by 79 in.

For the top dimensions, I figured 31 in. wide by 84 in. long. The top extends beyond the base so that the two 9-in. leaves can hang below. When down, the leaves allow for chairs to be slid under them. With the leaves up, the total width of the table-top becomes roughly 48 in. (because of the rule-joint overlap). I made this tabletop $^{13}/_{16}$ in. thick, but ¾ in. is the minimum—less than that and the quirk (or filet) on the leaf rule joint becomes too thin or fragile.

Glue Up the Top and Build the Base

Start by gluing up the top and leaves from ⅞-in.-thick stock. When flattened and sanded, the finished product is $^{13}/_{16}$ in. thick, a smidge more than minimum. Next, cut the legs to 1⅞ in. square by 29¼ in. long. Taper the four legs to 1⅜ in. on the table-saw using a jig, then clean them up on the jointer.

The mortises in the 4-in.-wide aprons are ⅜ in. thick by 1⅛ in. deep by 3⅛ in. wide (located ¾ in. from the top of the

Cherry Dining Table

This classic Shaker dining table features drop leaves that are supported by spinners cut into the aprons. For two other leaf-support options, see p. 7.

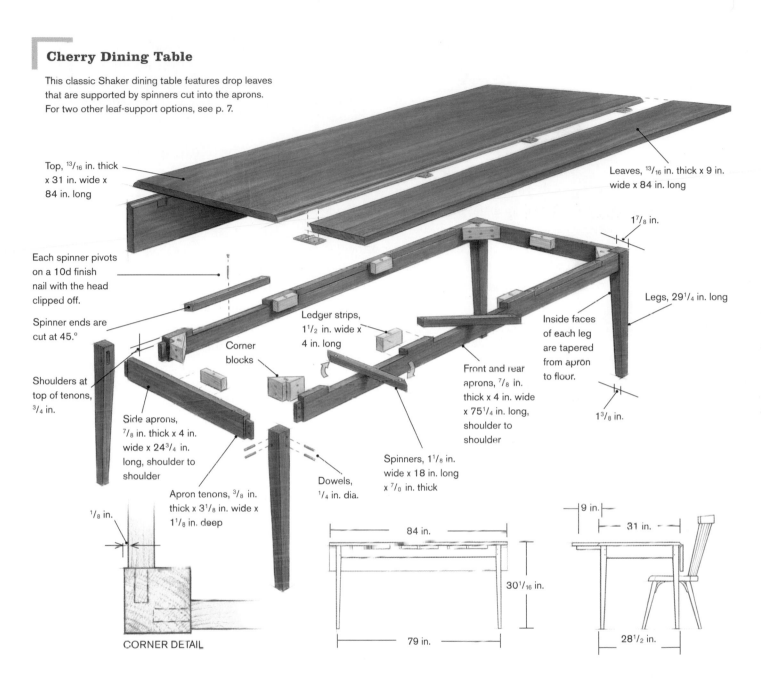

Top, $^{13}/_{16}$ in. thick x 31 in. wide x 84 in. long

Leaves, $^{13}/_{16}$ in. thick x 9 in. wide x 84 in. long

$1^7/_8$ in.

Each spinner pivots on a 10d finish nail with the head clipped off.

Spinner ends are cut at 45.°

Legs, $29^1/_4$ in. long

Ledger strips, $1^1/_2$ in. wide x 4 in. long

Corner blocks

Inside faces of each leg are tapered from apron to floor.

$1^3/_8$ in.

Shoulders at top of tenons, $^3/_4$ in.

Side aprons, $^7/_8$ in. thick x 4 in. wide x $24^3/_4$ in. long, shoulder to shoulder

Front and rear aprons, $^7/_8$ in. thick x 4 in. wide x $75^1/_4$ in. long, shoulder to shoulder

Spinners, $1^1/_8$ in. wide x 18 in. long x $^7/_8$ in. thick

Dowels, $^1/_4$ in. dia.

Apron tenons, $^3/_8$ in. thick x $3^1/_8$ in. wide x $1^1/_8$ in. deep

$^1/_8$ in.

CORNER DETAIL

9 in.

31 in.

84 in.

$30^1/_{16}$ in.

79 in.

$28^1/_2$ in.

leg and ⅛ in. from the apron bottom). I'm fortunate enough to own a horizontal slot mortiser, but this joint is easily cut by hand, with a drill press and chisels or with a router.

The aprons are milled from ⅞-in.-thick stock: two pieces 4 in. by 28 in. and two pieces 4¼ in. by 79 in. (The long side aprons are purposely oversize in both dimensions.) Before you cut and chop up the long aprons to make the leaf supports, or spinners, make a story stick. The stick shows the location of the two legs, the

three spinners, the four hinges, and the four attachment points where the top will be screwed to the base. With the story stick, you can then make witness marks in the appropriate locations on the aprons: two short 3-in. ends, three 18-in. spinners, and two spacers between the spinners. Then rip 1¼-in.-wide strips the full length of both aprons and joint the pieces. With the witness marks in place, cut the spinners and the spacers to length with the miter gauge set to 45° (for other leaf-support options, see p. 7).

LET IT SPIN ON A NAIL. Becksvoort uses nails to act as pivot pins, because they are stronger than brass and can be let into a smaller hole.

Now it's time to reconstruct. Starting from the center, line up the spinner with its witness marks. On either side, glue and tape the two spacers onto the apron, place the other two spinners, and glue the two end spacers. Then remove the spinners and clamp the spacers. Drill ⅛-in. holes through the centerpoints of each of the six spinners. Once the glue has dried, attach the spinners using 10d finish nails. Let the heads protrude about ¼ in. and nip them off with pliers. Then sand the aprons, cut them to length, and cut all of the tenons.

Now glue the long aprons to the legs and pin the joints with ¼-in.-dia. pins. When the two long sides of the table are ready, glue and pin the short aprons between them.

With the base assembled, make corner blocks from 1¾-in. by 3½-in. stock to strengthen the joint. Screw each block into both the aprons and leg. The aprons are only ⅞ in. thick, so add 1½-in.-wide ledger strips to the top inside surfaces between the spinners. These ledgers are drilled out for a ¼-in. by ⅜-in. slot to allow for movement of the top. Near each leg, there is also a similar slot in the corner blocks, as well as a 1-in.-dia. access hole on the bottom of

the blocks. On the end aprons, add a ledger strip with just a ¼-in.-dia. hole at the center. These two holes anchor the tabletop and ensure even wood movement across the top.

Cut the Rule Joint

Once you've established the critical dimensions of the rule joint (see the sidebar on p. 8), it's time to set up the router. I have two, so I can have one set up for the roundover cut (table edge) and the other for the cove cut (leaf). That allows me to go back and recut either portion of the joint if I'm not happy with the fit.

Make the roundover cuts first on the tabletop. Three passes usually get me to the appropriate depth. The router bit's bearing rides on just a sliver of edge on the final pass, so you need to clamp an auxiliary wood fence to the router base for a longer bearing surface.

Next, mount a cove bit in the router and make three passes under each leaf. Now fit each leaf next to the tabletop, and sight down the joint. Differences in height will, for the most part, be pulled together by the four hinges. Differences in width or parallelism will have to be adjusted. First use a

---

1 CUT THE SPINNERS FROM THE APRON

CUT APART THE APRON. At the tablesaw, rip the spinner stock from the top edge of the apron.

SEPARATE THE SPINNER STOCK. Becksvoort cuts the spinners using a 45° crosscut sled.

2 REASSEMBLE THE APRON

POSITION THE SPINNERS. Starting at the center of the apron, clamp the first spinner in place.

block plane to remove tight areas (usually on the leaf, which is more prone to bowing). Once the gap between leaf and table is a constant width, flip over the leaf and rerout the cove. Because the bearing rides on the quirk that you've just planed to fit, that's where all of the routing takes place. Once you're satisfied with the fit of both joints, you can install the hinges.

Attach Leaves and Fine-Tune the Fit

First, locate the hinges using the story stick. Because the hinges are perfectly flush to the underside (if properly installed), the locations can be altered if you have a severe warp in a leaf, for example. However, if your table is narrow, and you have attachment screws that go through the aprons, the hinges cannot go in the same place as the screws. Bring a line from the quirk on the tabletop to the underside of the table. Set a marking gauge $1/64$ in. closer to the table's edge and mark through all eight hinge locations. Then center the hinge pins over the scribe marks, with the long leaves extending onto the table leaves. With a pencil, mark the locations of the hinge barrels and draw these lines parallel to the scribe marks.

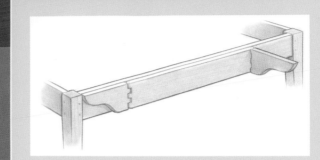

Other Leaf-Support Options

Swing Arms

Swing arms involve a double apron along the leaf sides. Knuckle joints on both ends of the short apron allow the ends to swing out to support the leaves. With proper spacing and planning, one or more swing arms can be used. With well-made knuckle joints, this is arguably the strongest leaf-support system because it does not involve cutting the apron.

Sliding Supports

Although a bit more work than making spinners, sliding supports are a neat and clean alternative. They should be no more than a third the height of the aprons. They work best where the leaves are less than half the width of the tabletop.

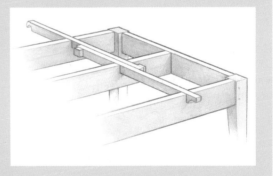

3 ATTACH THE SPINNERS

REBUILD THE APRON. Reglue the parts of the apron, making sure everything remains in the correct order. Keep things tight, and work from the center toward the ends.

DON'T JUST DRIVE A NAIL. With the spinner clamped in place, drill a hole in the center to accept a 10d finish nail.

BUMPERS ALLOW SMOOTH SPINNING. Before installing the spinners, Becksvoort planes them slightly, then sets nylon bumpers into place.

CUT HALF A RULE JOINT. Take several light passes before setting the bit to final depth and cutting the roundover portion of the rule joint. Then cut the leaf of the tabletop in several passes with a cove bit.

Using a ¼-in. bit, rout out for the hinge barrel. This trough can be a bit deeper and wider than the barrel, but no longer. Clean the ends with a ¼-in. chisel. Clamp both ends of the table and leaves right at the joint. Place the hinge barrel into the trough, keep the pin centered on the scribe line,

and use a sharp knife to scribe all four sides of the hinge. With the router set to the thickness of the leaves, rout the mortise and clean the corners with a chisel. The hinge should be snug and flush. Drive in all six screws (at least ⅛ in. shorter than the top thickness). Repeat for each hinge.

The Rule Joint: It All Hinges on the Barrel

When hinging a rule joint, convention says to center the hinge under the quirk, but I've found that it's better to offset the center of the hinge $1/64$ in. closer to the edge of the tabletop. The center of the hinge pin is buried $1/8$ in. above the bottom surface, which is the rotating axis of the joint. Consequently, the quirk height is the sum of the depth of the hinge pin ($1/8$ in.) plus the radius of the roundover bit ($1/2$ in.), which totals $5/8$ in., subtracted from the total thickness of the top. To keep the quirks substantial, I made this tabletop $1^3/16$ in. thick, but $3/4$ in. is the minimum. For a $1^3/16$-in.-thick top, that leaves a $3/16$-in. quirk on the tabletop. On the leaf, a $1/32$-in. clearance is ideal between it and the table, meaning that the leaf quirk is only $5/32$ in.

LOCATE THE HINGE BARREL. Square a line up from the quirk.

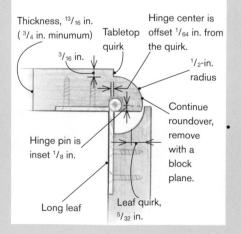

Rule Joint Detail

Thickness, $13/16$ in. ($3/4$ in. minumum)

Tabletop quirk

$3/16$ in.

Hinge center is offset $1/64$ in. from the quirk.

$1/2$-in. radius

Continue roundover, remove with a block plane.

Hinge pin is inset $1/8$ in.

Long leaf

Leaf quirk, $5/32$ in.

MARK THE CONTACT SPOTS. Set the leaf in place and mark spots where the joint makes contact.

TRIM THE LEAF, not the tabletop. A few passes with a handplane helps achieve an even reveal. Once the joint closes up, rerout the profile on the leaf and try another test fit.

If the table and leaves are straight, fitted, and laid out accurately, fine-tuning the joint is a minor chore. I fold down the leaf and take a few passes with a block plane along the bottom edge of the top. A bit of hand-sanding, and that's it. Frequently, it is a bit more involved. When I fold the leaf back up, it invariably rubs and squeaks. Often I can visually locate the points of contact and eliminate them with a rabbet plane and sandpaper. More often than not, I get out my supply of ancient carbon paper and slide it between the leaf and table, then fold the leaf up and down a few times to locate the friction points. I do this along the entire length, two or three times, planing and sanding the dark spots each time.

When both leaves fold smoothly, mark equal distances from the end hinges for an 84-in. length, square a line across both ends, and cut the assembly to length. I use a circular saw with a fence clamped in place. I belt-sand through to 320 grit, hand-sand using 320 grit, and then polish with 0000 steel wool.

Attach the top, open the spinners 90°, and mark under the tabletop for stops. A small ½-in. by ½-in. by 1 in. block glued to each of the six marked locations allows the spinners to open perpendicular to the table

3 **INSTALL THE HINGES AND CHECK THE FIT**

CARBON PAPER STILL HAS A USE. Becksvoort holds carbon paper between the joint as he opens and closes the leaf. Black marks are left where the joint is too tight. Those spots are trimmed with sandpaper or a block plane.

aprons. If I detect any sag in the leaves, I glue a small wedge-shaped shim in front of the stop blocks to level the leaves.

My finish of choice is Tried & True varnish oil, four or five coats applied over a three-week period. Rub with 0000 steel wool after the first coat, and let subsequent coats build to a satin sheen.

CHRISTIAN BECKSVOORT is a contributing editor to *Fine Woodworking* magazine.

Pembroke Table

Divorce is a nasty thing. Aside from the obvious casualty of the demise of my family, I regret the fact that Eddie will no longer be my father-in-law. Over the course of nearly 26 years, he has become one of my best friends. He always admired a Pembroke table I'd made years ago, and in fact, he commented on it almost every time he came to our house. In appreciation for all that I've learned from

him—he'd been more than a surrogate father since my dad died—I wanted to make another one of the tables for him.

Pembroke tables have been around for centuries. Small and graceful, they have been made in forms simple to elaborate. The one I made is on the simple side—the only adornments being the tapered legs and the curved top. What makes the table fun to build are the moving parts: the hinged drop leaves with their attendant rule joints and the short, wood-hinged arms that support the leaves. In the drawings, I've included the dimensions for my table, which is 34¾ in. long at the center of the top. You can adjust the dimensions of the table to suit your needs. Most often, Pem-

DROP-LEAF RULE JOINT and wood-hinged leaf supports are fussy but fun.

broke tables are small side tables, but they were built in all sizes. I once measured an antique Pembroke table with a 48-in.-long top.

Two-Piece Jig Is Used to Taper Legs on the Tablesaw

I can't claim ever to have had an original thought, and I certainly can't claim to have invented anything as far as woodworking is concerned. The tapering jig I used for the table's legs is no exception. I borrowed the idea from Charles Grivas of West Cornwall, Connecticut. I'm not sure he invented it, either, but it sure works well.

The tapered legs are cut from 1%16-in. square billets, 29¾ in. long (see the photos at right). The taper starts 6 in. down from the top of each leg. The legs taper on all sides to ⅞ in. at the floor. It's a good idea to cut the mortises in the legs before you start tapering.

Set your tablesaw fence for about 5 in. and rip two 35-in.-long medium-density fiberboard (MDF) or plywood scraps. After ripping, don't touch that tablesaw. You're going to taper the billets by setting them proud of the edge of the ripped strips and sending them through the tablesaw at the same fence setting, once for each tapered leg side, for a total of four cuts.

Lay out a ⅞-in. square centered on the bottom end of one of the billets and square around the billet 6 in. down from the top. Set the billet atop one of the MDF strips with the 6-in. square line and the outside edge of the ⅞-in. square flush with the edge of the MDF.

Trace the billet onto the MDF and then, using a bandsaw or jigsaw, remove the outline of the billet. After you've made the cut in the MDF, pressure-fit the billet into the cutout and then send the MDF through the tablesaw.

Hold the one-taper billet to the edge of the second MDF strip, just as you did

Tapered Legs

THE LEG TAPERING JIG is made from two strips of MDF ripped to the same width. The edge of a ⅞ -in. square marked on the bottom of a leg billet hangs over the edge of the MDF strip. The billet, held to the outside edge of the smaller square, is traced on the MDF and cut away to make a pattern for the first two cuts on the four-taper legs. Leg billets are pressure-fit into the cutouts in the MDF and ripped on the tablesaw.

RIP THE FIRST TWO TAPERS ON ONE JIG. The part of the billet that sits proud of the MDF strip is ripped away when the MDF strip is sent through the saw at the same setting at which the strips were ripped.

COLOR CODING CAN COUNTER CONFUSION. The author marked two perpendicular sides of each billet end with a red pen for the first cuts and a green pen for the second cuts. The jigs are coded the same way. (The first cuts in the billet in the photo have already been sawn away.)

before. One edge of the ⅞-in. leg-bottom square will have been removed by the first cut. Line up the 6-in. square line again and the edge of the ⅞-in. square opposite the side that was removed with the first cut. Trace the one-taper leg onto the second strip of MDF and remove the leg outline as you did before. To distinguish the two MDF strips, and thus to avoid cutting the wrong tapers on the wrong sides—I've been known to make mistakes in my life   I made a red mark on the first-taper strip and a green mark on the other. Then I marked the end of the billets: red for the first cuts and green for the second cuts.

When you have made the cutouts on both MDF strips, you're ready to taper. Fit

Hinged Swinging Leaf Support

THE DROP-LEAF SUPPORTS SWING ON A WOOD HINGE. Hinge knuckles–two on the support and three on the stationary piece–are ⅝ in. long. The width of each knuckle is determined by the width of the apron stock divided into five parts. A cyma curve on the end of each support adds a decorative touch.

KNUCKLE RELIEF. The back of the wood hinge knuckles are cut away at an angle so that the hinge can swing freely. If the knuckles were left square, their front sides would pinch one another as they swung.

FIT TO BE DRILLED. Once the wood hinges have been pared to fit, clamp the pieces together against a backer board and drill a ⅛-in.-dia. hole through the hinge. A ⅛-in.-dia. steel rod is used as a hinge pin.

FINGERHOLD IS CUT WITH A GOUGE. The swinging-leaf support, cut on the end with a gentle cyma curve, nests against the apron end, which gets cut with a slightly more exaggerated curve. The back of the support is relieved with a gouge to provide a fingerhold for opening the support.

a billet into the first-taper strip and taper the first side. Then turn the billet and taper a side perpendicular to the first. Fit the billet into the second MDF strip and taper the two remaining perpendicular sides.

Swinging Leaf Support Pivots on a Wood Hinge

The table's short leaves are supported by flipperlike arms that swing out of the side aprons on wood hinges and fold flush into the aprons when the leaves are down. The five-knuckle wood hinge is pinned at the centerline of the side apron with a length of ⅛-in.-dia. steel rod. Cut two lengths of 4½-in.-wide stock 6 in. longer than the finished length of the aprons. You'll need the extra length to account for the tenons and the wood you waste when making the hinge.

Mark five knuckles of the same size across the apron's width. Crosscut the apron stock through the five knuckle lines and then make a mark ⅝ in. from each end of the cut. In ¾-in. stock, a ⅝-in.-long

knuckle works well. Anything longer and the hinge will bind when it's glued to the secondary-wood subapron. The swinging leaf support has two knuckles, and the stationary apron piece has three knuckles. Butt the two marked pieces end to end and mark waste lines on each piece (see the left photo above).

Cutting the wood hinges is exacting. To look good, the knuckles must fit tightly but should not be so tight that the hinge won't swing. Prepare to do a lot of test fitting. The back side of the hinges must be relieved at about a 45° angle so that the knuckles on one piece can swing past the knuckles on the other (see the photo second from left above).

Once the knuckles fit together, clamp the two pieces to a backer board and drill a ⅛-in.-dia. hole through the center of all of the knuckles (see the photo second from right on the facing page). Push a long piece of ⅛-in.-dia. steel rod through the hinge and test the action. Unless you're a real ace, you'll have to pare away at the knuckles to

TABLE APRONS ARE DOUBLE THICK. After the swinging leaf support has been cut, fit, and drilled and the end of the apron is cut with a cyma curve, the primary apron pieces are glued to subaprons. Cutting tenons on the doubled-up aprons is straightforward. In the photo, the swinging support has been removed from the apron.

METAL PIN, WOOD HINGE. The top of the pin is peened to prevent it from slipping out. In operation, the swinging leaf support folds flat against the apron when the table leaves are down.

get the hinge to swing smoothly. Using a piece of long rod for the test fitting makes it easy to pull out the pin when you have to adjust the knuckles.

Each swinging leaf support has a gentle cyma curve cut into the end, and it folds flat against another, slightly more exaggerated curve cut into the apron end. Use a gouge to relieve part of the back of the leaf support to provide a fingerhold (see the right photo on the facing page).

When you are convinced that the leaf support works smoothly, and you're pleased with the fairness of the curves cut on the supports and apron ends, glue the stationary part of the hinge and the apron end to a 4½-in.-wide subapron made of a second-ary wood (poplar in this table). Because the primary apron is broken by the swinging leaf support, the subapron gives strength to the assembly. Gluing the apron pieces together makes it easy to cut the tenons (see the photo above).

Rule Joints Add Decorative Touch

The hinged leaves on some unadorned drop-leaf tables simply butt to the tops when folded up. Rule joints—a combination of two moldings, cove and roundover—add a decorative and a structural element to a drop-leaf table. When a table leaf is folded down and hangs vertically from the tabletop, you see a decorative, molded roundover along the edge of the top. And when the leaf is folded up, the cove in the leaf rests on and is supported by the roundover, giving strength to the joint when the table is loaded.

For the first Pembroke table I made, I borrowed rule-joint planes from Mike

Mahogany Pembroke Table

Traditionally, Pembroke tables have a wide top and shallow leaves. With the leaves open, this table's top appears almost circular with spurs making four corners. When the leaves are folded down, the spurs line up with the outside edges of the tapered legs. The leaves are held open with swinging leaf supports.

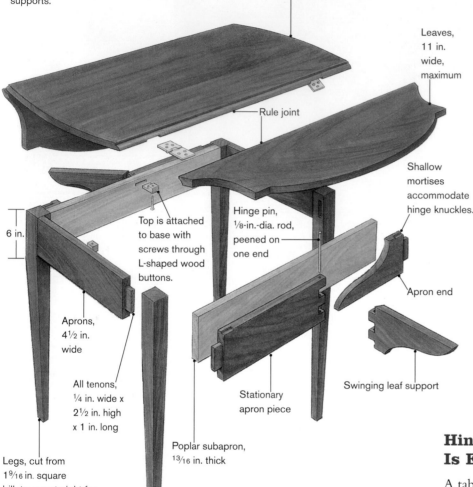

Top, 34¾ in. wide x 17¾ in. long, maximum

Leaves, 11 in. wide, maximum

Rule joint

Shallow mortises accommodate hinge knuckles.

6 in.

Top is attached to base with screws through L-shaped wood buttons.

Hinge pin, ⅛-in.-dia. rod, peened on one end

Apron end

Aprons, 4½ in. wide

All tenons, ¼ in. wide x 2½ in. high x 1 in. long

Stationary apron piece

Swinging leaf support

Legs, cut from 1⁹⁄₁₆ in. square billets, are straight for 6 in., then taper on all sides to ⅞ in. at the bottom.

Poplar subapron, ¹³⁄₁₆ in. thick

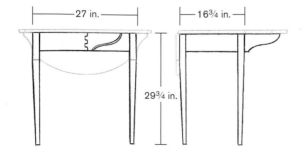

27 in.

16¾ in.

29¾ in.

Dunbar, and in fact, the inspiration for this table came from his Taunton Press book, *Federal Furniture* (1986). Cutting the joint with molding planes wasn't easy; using a router table with a ½-in. cove bit and a ½-in. roundover bit was a piece of cake.

I don't think it matters whether you first cut the cove in the leaves or the roundover in the top. What's important is that you have a perfectly jointed edge between leaves and top before you cut the moldings. It's also important that the fillets—the flat, vertical section of each molding—above the roundover and the cove be the same dimension. If they aren't, the top and the leaves won't sit flush in the opened position. I used ³⁄₁₆-in. fillets on my table.

Trust me on this: It's a good idea to run extra lengths of scrap with the cove and roundovers run into the edges. Table-leaf hinges are a different breed of (swinging) cat, and it's a good idea to mount a pair to some scraps before you attack the real top. And later, the scraps can come in handy for tuning up the rule joints.

Hinge Installation Is Exacting

A table-leaf hinge is unusual for several reasons: One leaf is longer than the other; the leaves are countersunk opposite the barrel; and in operation, the hinge folds away from the barrel rather than around it as it does on a regular butt hinge. The longer side of the hinge gets screwed to the table leaf.

Rule-jointed table leaves pivot not from the tabletop's widest point but rather from a point in line with the fillet on the roundover (see the drawing on the facing page). The exacting part of setting a tabletop hinge comes in setting the hinge barrel (and thus the pivot point) in line with the fillet. If you set the pivot point a little too far forward or too far back, the rule joint will bind as it swings or the leaf will hang too low, revealing the hinge mortise. Neither case is the end of the world, and both can be remedied with a little fiddling.

Mounting a table hinge requires that the hinge barrel get mortised deep into the tabletop and the hinge body get mortised flush with both the tabletop and the leaves. Transcribe the fillet line—½ in. back from the edge of the roundover—to the underside of the top. Use a ¼-in. chisel to knock out a rough mortise for the barrel, centering the hinge pin on the line you've transcribed. Neatness doesn't count here because the hinge body will cover the barrel mortise. Once the barrel has been mortised and the hinge body rests flush with the underside of the top and leaf, you can mark around the hinge and then cut the mortise for the hinge body into the top and the leaves. Drill holes for one screw in each of the hinge leaves and attach the leaves to the top.

Set the top and leaves on the edge of your bench so that one of the leaves hangs over the side, and test the action of the hinges and the rule joint. It's likely that you'll have to fuss with the joints to get them just right. If the leaf hangs too low on either side or both, such that you see the hinge mortise on the underside of the tabletop, you'll have to deepen the hinge-barrel mortise on the tabletop. Don't deepen the end of the mortise on the edge of the roundover, just the barrel mortise and that area of the hinge leaf toward the center of the tabletop; you're trying to sink the hinge deeper into the tabletop and thus raise the height of the attached leaf.

If the leaf binds as it swings open—you'll hear an annoying squeaking, scraping noise—the easiest thing to do is get out the sandpaper. I used spray adhesive to attach a

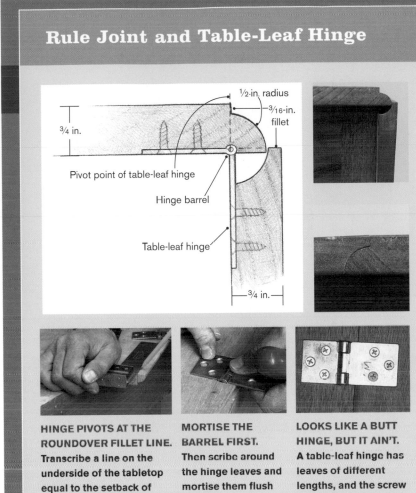

Rule Joint and Table-Leaf Hinge

½-in. radius
³/₁₆-in. fillet
¾ in.
Pivot point of table-leaf hinge
Hinge barrel
Table-leaf hinge
¾ in.

HINGE PIVOTS AT THE ROUNDOVER FILLET LINE. Transcribe a line on the underside of the tabletop equal to the setback of the vertical fillet on the rule joint.

MORTISE THE BARREL FIRST. Then scribe around the hinge leaves and mortise them flush with the tabletop.

LOOKS LIKE A BUTT HINGE, BUT IT AIN'T. A table-leaf hinge has leaves of different lengths, and the screw holes are countersunk on the sides opposite the barrel.

strip of sandpaper to one of the test scraps I made when cutting the rule joint. Use the scrap with the cove cut into it to sand the roundover and vice versa. When both leaves swing well, drill and drive in the rest of the screws.

Trammels Lay Out the Top

When viewed from above, the top of the table looks like a circle with squared-off spurs at each corner. In fact, the edges of the table ends and the leaves are sections of a circumference, each with a different centerpoint. To my eye, one of the cool things about the table is the way the spurs

Laying Out the Tabletop

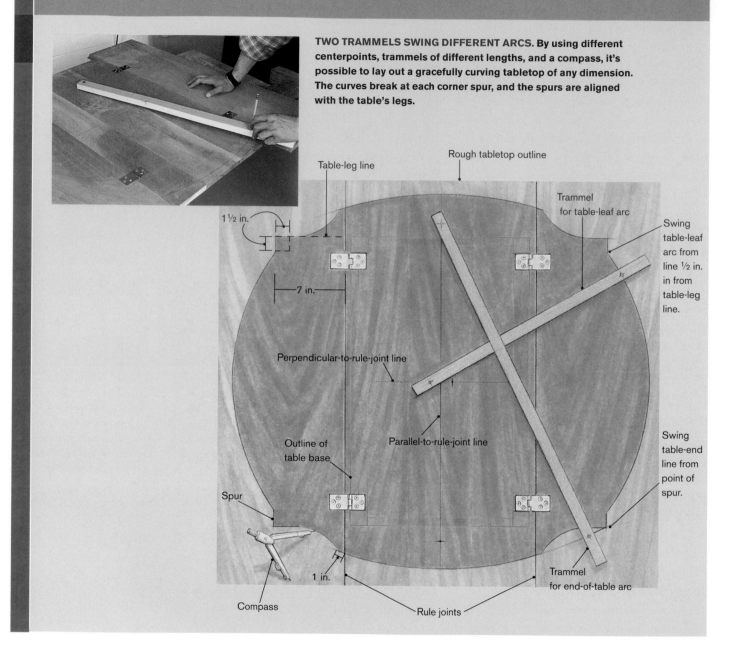

TWO TRAMMELS SWING DIFFERENT ARCS. By using different centerpoints, trammels of different lengths, and a compass, it's possible to lay out a gracefully curving tabletop of any dimension. The curves break at each corner spur, and the spurs are aligned with the table's legs.

Rough tabletop outline

Table-leg line

Trammel for table-leaf arc

Swing table-leaf arc from line ½ in. in from table-leg line.

1½ in.

7 in.

Perpendicular-to-rule-joint line

Parallel-to-rule-joint line

Outline of table base

Swing table-end line from point of spur.

Spur

1 in.

Trammel for end-of-table arc

Compass

Rule joints

on the leaves hang even with the outside edges of the legs.

With the hinges mounted and the rule joints tuned, flip the top over on your bench and find the center of the top. Mark two long axis lines through the centerpoint, one line perpendicular to the rule joint and one parallel to it. Temporarily set the table base upside down on the top, clamp the leaves against the legs, and mark lines on the underside of the tabletop along the outside of the four legs (see the drawing above). It's a good idea to make witness lines so that you can align the table base and the top the same way in the future.

On each table-leg line, mark a point 7 in. from the rule joint. This point will become the end of the spur. Traditionally, Pembroke tables have short leaves, and although the 7-in. point is arbitrary, it's a good size for the leaves.

From that 7-in. point, mark a 1½-in.-long line perpendicular to the table-leg line, and then mark a point 1½ in. back toward the rule joint on the table-leg line. These 1½-in. squared corners will become the four spurs. Now you'll draw sections of circles between the spurs.

I made a trammel out of a pencil and a strip of wood with a drywall screw through one end (see the photo on the facing page). The radii you mark on the top will vary based on the size of the table base you've made and the rough width and length of your tabletop and leaves. To lay out the curve on the table ends, use the parallel-to-the-rule-joint axis line you made through the top's centerpoint. To lay out the curves for the leaves, use the perpendicular line.

First the table ends: Moving the drywall screw point along the parallel line adjusts the radius of the circle you swing from the tips of the spurs. Setting the screw point closer to the center of the table will make a tighter circle, and if you move it farther away, you will make a wider circle.

Hold the trammel so that the drywall screw sticks in the parallel line and the other end rests on one of the spurs. Swing the pencil end of the trammel in an arc to the spur on the opposite side of the table. Move the screw up and down the parallel line and swing arcs with different radii until you find one that's pleasing to your eye. When you find a radius you like, mark the nonscrew end of the trammel and drill a hole in the stick so that you can pressure-fit a pencil through it. With the pencil through the stick, draw the circumference from the tip of one spur to the tip of the spur on the opposite side of the tabletop. To swing the same arc on the other end of the table, set the screw point the same distance from the tabletop centerpoint in the other direction.

For both table leaves, you are going to swing an arc using the perpendicular-to-the-rule-joint axis line you drew through the center of the tabletop. And this time, instead of swinging an arc from the tips of one of the spurs, you'll swing the arc from the end of the 1½-in. line that's perpendicular to the table-leg line.

The last thing to do in laying out the tabletop is to relieve the corners of the table-end arcs. Relieving the corners adds to the illusion that the top is a true circle. Using a compass, swing a pleasing arc from a point on the table-end arc 1 in. past the line where the leaf meets the top to the point you've marked 1½ in. down the table-leg line.

After cutting out the tabletop with a jigsaw, I planed, scraped, and sanded it until I was blue in the face. I used 340-grit sandpaper to knock the sharp edges off the tabletop and base, wanting to maintain the crisp corners. To accommodate the drop-leaf-hinge barrels and to make the tabletop lie flat on the base, I knocked out a small mortise on the base under each barrel. To attach the top to the base, I used small, L-shaped wood buttons that screw to the underside of the top and fit into chiseled slots in the base.

I was going to use an oil-and-shellac finish on the table, but after the first coat of oil, I didn't like the way it looked on the mahogany, so I'll probably scrape it off and go for a straight shellac finish. Hey, we all make mistakes; we all change our minds. Look what happened to my marriage. I just hope that my ex-father-in-law hasn't changed his mind about Pembroke tables.

JEFFERSON KOLLE is an editor at The Taunton Press.

One-Drawer Lamp Stand

BY MIKE DUNBAR

BUILD THIS HEPPLEWHITE TABLE and further hone your hand-tool skills.

This small table is a typical example of a furniture form that became popular in the 1790s and remained in favor through the first half of the 1800s. It is generally referred to by antique collectors as a lamp stand. That name distinguishes it from the tripod tables that had been popular during much of the 1700s. The name also explains this form's sudden development. Tripod stands are commonly called candle stands, from the practice of placing candlesticks on them to illuminate a room. Oil lamps became popular around 1790. But the lamps used highly combustible liquid fuel and so were more hazardous than a single candle flame.

To provide a more stable and safer resting place for oil lamps, the small, four-legged table was introduced. Outside the antique world, this form is called an end table, indicating the table's popular use at the ends of a sofa or on both sides of a bed. For this reason, many people prefer these tables in pairs. The pair I made is of woods native to New Hampshire—cherry with a curly maple veneer drawer front.

Making one of these tables is an excellent project to help the beginner or intermediate woodworker develop and practice hand-tool skills. It is a natural progression from the more basic joints and work methods used in creating a blanket chest. Obviously, this table could be built with straightforward machine work, but it is a lot more fun if you do at least some of the tasks by hand. You could prepare the stock with planes and handsaws, as I did when I made the blanket chest; however, for the table I did all of the thicknessing and ripping on machines. Then I moved to the bench to make the actual table. After stock preparation, the table has four major operations—the joinery, the leg taper, the top, and the drawer.

Backsaw Basics

SAW BOTH CORNERS, THEN CONNECT THE CUTS. Cutting through a tenon's long grain can be a problem unless you ease into it by making a diagonal cut through both corners and then connecting those cuts across the middle. Use the same process when cutting the shoulder.

Complete One Operation at a Time

The two most important tools you will use in making this table are the square and straightedge. Slight differences that are easy to overlook in a larger piece are magnified in a table this small. Use the straightedge and square to check everything as you progress.

After cutting all of the parts to size, remove any saw, planer, and jointer marks (if you used these machines) and obtain a smooth surface with handplanes. Check to be sure that with all of your handplane work, you do not plane out of square.

A mortise gauge is a scribing tool with two points and is used for laying out mortises and tenons. Adjust the two points to the width of the joint, and slide the fence to the thickness of the shoulder. Always run the gauge's fence against the outside surface on all parts. Doing so will give you a consistent reference that might not be reliable if you were to make some marks off the inside edges and some off the outside edges.

Use a square—again, always on the outside surface—to mark the ends of the mortises and the tenon shoulders. I lay out

TABLETOP ATTACHMENT. Use a marking gauge to mark ½ in. down from the top edge of the aprons and then use a gouge to cut pockets for the tabletop attachment screws.

the mortises so that the rails will protrude above the tops of the legs by 1/16 in. After the table has been glued up, it is easier to true the rail-to-leg joints by planing the long grain of the rails rather than trying to plane the end grain of the top of the legs.

Notice that the tenons used to join the rails to the legs have just one shoulder (see the drawings on p. 20). In keeping with the Federal period's preference for sleek lines, the rails are flush with the legs. If the tenons were double shouldered, the outside walls of the mortises would be too thin. While the single-shouldered tenons are not as resistant to racking, they are more than adequate for this table. They are also easier to cut.

Cherry Lamp Stand With Curly Maple Drawer Front

First popularized at the end of the 18th century, tables of this type are often made in pairs and used on both sides of a bed or couch. Plain in form, almost stark, this table is dressed up by the addition of curly maple veneer and cock beading on the drawer front. For cock-beading details, see the drawing on p. 26.

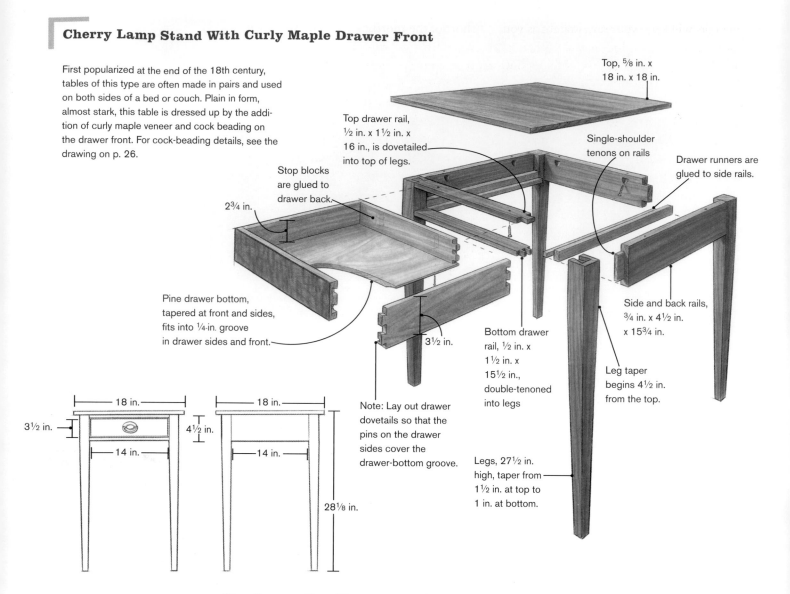

Top, ⅝ in. x 18 in. x 18 in.

Top drawer rail, ½ in. x 1½ in. x 16 in., is dovetailed into top of legs.

Single-shoulder tenons on rails

Drawer runners are glued to side rails.

Stop blocks are glued to drawer back.

2¾ in.

Pine drawer bottom, tapered at front and sides, fits into ¼-in. groove in drawer sides and front.

3½ in.

Bottom drawer rail, ½ in. x 1½ in. x 15½ in., double-tenoned into legs

Side and back rails, ¾ in. x 4½ in. x 15¾ in.

Leg taper begins 4½ in. from the top.

Note: Lay out drawer dovetails so that the pins on the drawer sides cover the drawer-bottom groove.

Legs, 27½ in. high, taper from 1½ in. at top to 1 in. at bottom.

18 in.

3½ in.

14 in.

18 in.

4½ in.

14 in.

28⅛ in.

Backsaw the Tenons and Chisel Out the Mortises

I cut tenons with a sharp backsaw (see the top photos on p. 19). I prefer to cut on the outside edge of the line rather than on the line itself. This usually results in a bit of extra material. Remember the old maxim about wood being easy to remove but hard to put back on. The extra material is easy to trim away.

Start the sawing with the shoulder. Hold the part in a bench hook—an easy-to-make holding device that is very useful in handwork. You can use clamps, but they take more time. Rather than laying the saw across the part and cutting the shoulder at once, tilt the saw so that you start on one corner. Repeat on the other corner and then connect the cuts. Although I lay out my shoulders with a square, I cut them at a slight angle (1° or 2°) away from the tenon, which helps in obtaining a tight joint between the shoulder and the leg and eliminates a lot of work with the shoulder plane.

Cut the tenon's cheek by holding the rail upright in a vise. It is hard to keep the saw from wandering if you cut straight across the part and straight down the cheek. Once again, start the cut on one corner and deepen it on one side almost to the shoulder. Repeat on the other side. These two cuts will keep your saw straight as you complete the cheek. To separate the waste cleanly, you may have to deepen the shoulder cut to meet the cheek. Do this carefully because overcutting will weaken the tenon.

Before moving on to the leg mortises, cut the screw pockets in the inside upper edges of the rails. Use a scribe to mark the pockets' upper surfaces. With a gouge, hollow out the pockets (see the bottom photo on p. 19). Drill the screw holes at an angle that will exit through the rail's top edge.

To hold the legs while cutting the mortises, I like the two-clamp system shown in the photos below. When I need to knock out a reluctant chip from a mortise, all I have to do is loosen one clamp and pick up the leg.

A mortise chisel will make quick work of chopping a mortise. It is a stout tool designed to take a lot of pounding and levering. Make sure your chisel is sharp. Start the mortise back from the end and drive the chisel straight down. Pull it out and move about ⅜ in. down the mortise for the second cut. The chisel's wedge shape pops out a chip of wood the same width as the tool. Repeat along the mortise, stopping short of the other end.

Begin another, deeper pass along the now well-defined opening. It is important that the mortise be perpendicular to the leg. To avoid wandering to one side, check yourself with a square. Do this frequently in the beginning of the cut. You will probably discover that you tend to lean to one side or another. (I tend to push too far away and usually need to draw the handle toward me.) Very quickly you will develop the feel for vertical, and you will need to check yourself only once in a while.

During the second and subsequent passes, the chips do not easily pop out of the mortise. You have to lever them loose by pulling the chisel so that it rocks on its bevel. This pulling is the reason for stopping

short of the mortise's end. The waste will keep the chisel from crushing the end. As the mortise deepens, it becomes more difficult to get the chips out. They pry loose but stick in the mortise. Keep a thin chisel or screwdriver on hand to use as a pick.

Check the mortise's depth with a ruler. It speeds up the fitting if you go just a bit deeper than the tenon. Finally, use the chisel to make two cleaning cuts that bring the mortise's narrow ends up to the scribe lines.

Rotate the leg and cut the second mortise. You will find that it intersects the first. To avoid blowing out large pieces of wood from the wall of the first mortise, drive the chisel with less force as you near the full depth.

Getting the Right Fit

To ease the tenon's fit into its mortise, use a low-angle block plane to ease all of the

Mortising With a Chisel

  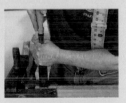

POPPING CHIPS. A stout mortise chisel is designed to be used as half cutting tool and half prybar. After driving the chisel into the wood with a mallet, you can pop the chip out of the hole. Don't try this with your bench chisels, or you might end up with a bent tool.

A SQUARE MORTISE MAKES A SQUARE TABLE. When you first mortise by hand, it is important to check your work constantly. Hold a square on the table leg and sight along the square and the edge of the chisel to make sure the mortise is square to the face of the leg.

MORTISE TUNING. If need be, use a wide chisel to pare the sides of a mortise when fitting it to an already-cut tenon. The author's two-clamp system holds a leg for mortising; the clamp flat on the bench is set just wider than the leg thickness, holding the leg securely but allowing it to be lifted out easily.

TRACING TAIL. The top drawer rail locks into the top end grain of the two front legs by means of a large dovetail. The bottom drawer rail is secured to the legs with two small tenons.

edges. Where necessary, trim the mortise wall. Use a wide, sharp chisel so that you can make the cut in a single pass, which creates a more uniform surface than trimming in multiple passes with a narrower chisel. This low-angle trimming is called paring. Where necessary, trim the tenon cheek with a shoulder plane. This plane's sides are square to the sole, and its narrow mouth allows it to take very controlled cuts. It is used cross-grain.

Repeat this process of fitting and trimming as necessary. You want a snug fit that will move by hand. You should not have to drive the tenon, and it should not fall out on its own. This friction fit may take a few tries to achieve, but hand skills develop only with practice. However, if you do trim too much, glue a piece of veneer to the tenon and start the trimming again.

When you can push the tenon to full depth, check the result. The shoulder should be tight to the leg. At the same time, check between the rail's lower edge and the leg for square. Do the same along the leg and the rail's outer surface. (This is easy to do before the legs are tapered and impossible afterward.) Make adjustments to the mortise or tenon as necessary. Use a shoulder plane to get a tight fit of the shoulder to the leg. Repeat the fitting until the table is standing on four legs. Do not be

too concerned if the rail's outer surface and the leg do not align perfectly. You will plane them after glue-up. Finally, fit the bottom drawer rail.

Lay out the dovetailed tenons that secure the top drawer rail to the front legs (see the photo above). Cut the tails using a backsaw the same way you did on the rail tenons. Start on one corner and cut down the line. Repeat on the other corner. Use the tails to lay out the pins on the top of the legs and fit and test the joints. Drill and countersink two top-attachment screw holes in the rail.

Dry-fit the table and clamp lightly. Test for square (see the top photo on the facing page). Double-check by measuring from corner to corner. Place the table on a flat surface such as a tablesaw to make sure all four legs will touch. Use a straightedge across all four top edges to look for high or low spots. Use a pair of winding sticks to test front to back and side to side. Winding sticks are two straightedges, usually of contrasting colors. When sighting across the winding sticks, you can make sure that all four sides are coplanar.

Legs Are Tapered with a Plane

Tapering a leg is very easy to do with a plane. On the lower end of each leg, measure in ¼ in. per side and connect the lines to make a square. On opposing surfaces of the leg, use a straightedge and pencil to connect the lines on the foot to the location of the rails' lower edges. Use a jack plane to remove the bulk of the waste, paying attention to the grain. Finish to the lines on both sides with a smoothing plane. Rotate the leg and do the same to the other sides. Then lay out the lines for the two remaining straight sides, and repeat the process. You cannot lay out all four sides at once because you would plane away the lines for the second two tapers while making the first two.

Glue and clamp up the table. When it is dry, clamp the table in a vise and plane the leg-to-rail joints flush, as necessary. Be careful, because the grain in the two parts runs in different directions, and any overlap by the plane will leave a rough cut on one surface or the other. Make sure your smoothing plane is very sharp and well tuned. Use a very low setting. If you do nick an adjacent surface with a cross-grain cut, clean it up with a handheld scraper.

The Top's Long Grain Runs Side to Side

For the table's top, you will probably have to glue up two or more pieces. Remember that the joint will run side to side so that you won't see end grain when looking at the table head-on. Make the top oversize and cut it to dimension when the glue is dry. The top is small, so the glue joint can be done very easily with a jointer plane. Although I did it while gluing up boards of the blanket chest, I don't recommend springing the joints for this tabletop because it is made of short, thin hardwood.

Once the glue is dry, joint and square one edge with a jointer plane. You can cut the other three sides on a tablesaw or with a fine handsaw. If you do it by hand, use a large square to lay out two edges square with the first. I had one of my medium-size

RULER AND SQUARE ARE INVALUABLE. After the joints have been cut, dry-fit the table with clamps and take diagonal measurements across the top of the frame (left). Equal diagonal measurements indicate it is square. Check the rail-to-leg joints for square while the table is clamped but before the legs are tapered (below).

handsaws filed to a 14-point crosscut for use on thin hardwood. Using this saw, there is almost no chipping on the lower edge. Measure 18 in. up these two sawn sides and lay out the final edge. Test again for square and make any final adjustments while smoothing the sawn edges with handplanes.

Use a jointer plane to remove saw marks from the two edges that are edge grain. A low-angle block plane with a very light setting will clean the end grain. You can do this with a bench plane if it is razor sharp. Be sure to plane in from both edges toward the middle to avoid chipping the corners.

Jack-plane the bottom to remove any planer marks, glue, or overlap. This surface

HEATING HIDE GLUE TURNS IT TO GOO. The pine drawer front is veneered with curly maple. Coat the drawer front with hot hide glue and coat both sides of the veneer, then stick the pieces together. Coating both sides of the veneer keeps the thin wood from curling.

DON'T HIT WITH A VENEER HAMMER. The hammer is used more like a squeegee. After the glue-coated veneer is placed on the glue-coated drawer front, use the veneer hammer, starting in the middle and working toward the edges, to push air bubbles out from between the two layers. The hide glue sets in a few minutes.

FLUSH-CUTTING VENEER SAW. The curved, thin blade of a veneer saw has no set to its teeth, making it ideal for flush-cutting across the drawer front's veneer. The saw will leave a crisp edge on the veneer's finished side.

is not seen, so there is no point in spending a lot of time on it. Use a smoothing plane on the top to remove any thickness-planer marks and any overlap in the joint. Finish up with a scraper to achieve a perfect surface. I have a Stanley No. 112 scraper plane (see "Sources" on p. 27) that I use to produce a glassy surface.

Place the table upside down on its top, protecting the top from damage during this process with a towel or blanket between it and the workbench. Measure to make sure you have the same amount of overhang

on all four edges. Once you have the best placement, make some light marks on the top's bottom surface with a pencil, just in case something moves while you are working. Screw the top in place.

The Drawer Has a Veneered Front

The drawer front is veneered with curly maple. If exposed, the edges of the veneer would easily chip when the drawer is opened and closed. The veneer is protected with an applied raised edge called cock beading (see the drawing and photos on p. 26). This detail serves another important purpose. With flush rails, the table is sleek to the point of being stark. Cock beading makes the front three-dimensional. The beading is usually the same wood as the table.

The cock beading on the drawer ends is narrower than that on the top and bottom. The end pieces are fit into rabbets cut across the dovetails. The tails would be weakened if the cock beading were run right up to the scribe line. Of course, the two different widths of the cock beading require the use of a stopped miter joint.

Make the drawer to fit the opening. Smooth-planing machine and saw marks and trimming the leg joints may have made very small changes to the dimensions in the drawing. I made the drawer of pine, as a New England cabinetmaker would have in the 18th century—a southern cabinetmaker

would have used poplar—but you can use any suitable wood.

Thickness the wood for the drawer, the runners, and the cock beading. Remove the planer marks with a smoothing plane. Then cut the parts to dimension. You can use a square to lay out these cuts, or you can use the edge of a bench hook as a guide. Glue the drawer runners to the lower inside edge of the rails. The glue will dry while you are making the other parts.

To make a drawer that slides smoothly and fits well, it is important to maintain square. For small parts, use a shooting board and a well-tuned and sharp handplane. I use a Stanley No. 605 in a shooting board. Its cutter is adjusted laterally so that its edge is at a right angle to the right check, ensuring that it cuts a square edge. After ripping the parts to width and crosscutting them to length, check for square. If they are not perfect, scribe a line with the striking knife

SCRAPER PLANE FOR DRAWER VENEER. After cutting the veneer flush with the drawer front, use a scraper plane to finish the veneer.

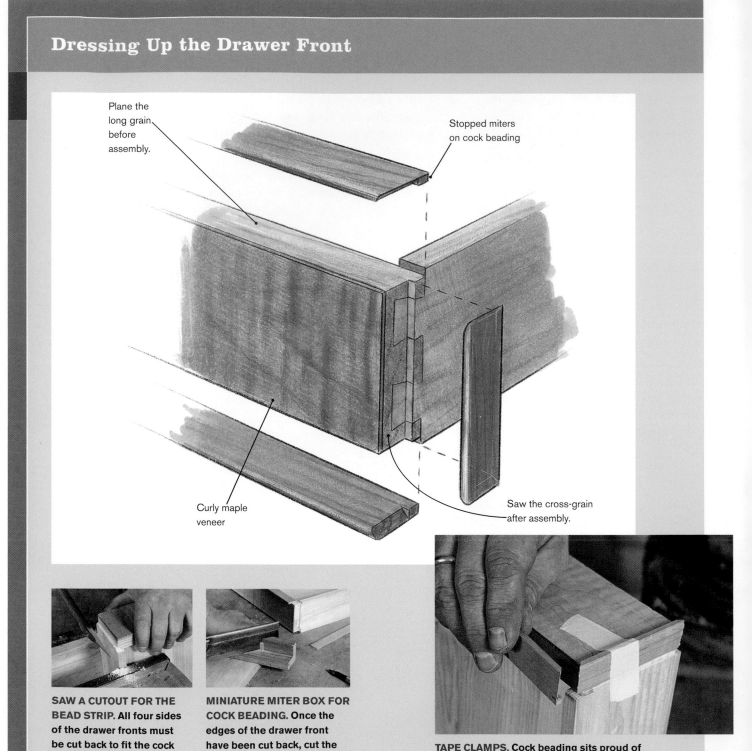

Plane the long grain before assembly.

Stopped miters on cock beading

Curly maple veneer

Saw the cross-grain after assembly.

SAW A CUTOUT FOR THE BEAD STRIP. All four sides of the drawer fronts must be cut back to fit the cock beading. Cut each end of the drawer with a backsaw and plane the top and bottom to size.

MINIATURE MITER BOX FOR COCK BEADING. Once the edges of the drawer front have been cut back, cut the cock beading with a backsaw and a small miter box.

TAPE CLAMPS. Cock beading sits proud of the veneer by ⅛ in. Masking tape works like another set of hands to hold the cock beading in place while fitting the final pieces. After all of the pieces have been fitted, glue and clamp the cock beading in place.

where they need to be trimmed. Place the pieces on the shooting board and use the plane to shave the end grain to the scribe line. Keep the high side toward the shooting board's stop so you do not chip the far edge.

Groove the sides and front for the drawer bottom. I did this using a plow plane, which is fast and easy. However, a plow plane is an expensive tool. If you do not have one, use your tablesaw.

When you lay out your dovetails, leave enough room above and below the tails to trim the top and bottom edges of the drawer front to accept the cock beading. Cut and fit the dovetails. When you are satisfied with the fit, run a marking gauge along the top and bottom edges of the front and plane to this line. Using the shooting board gives you good control, and because the scribed line is facing up, it is easier to see.

There are several ways to make a drawer bottom. I used the method favored by period New England cabinetmakers. They used a jack plane to feather the front edge and two sides until they were narrow enough to fit in the groove.

Use a bandsaw to cut two pieces of veneer from a piece of curly maple. That way, the grain pattern on this table and its mate will match each other. Between cuts, handplane the wood so that each sheet of veneer has one smooth face for gluing. I applied the veneer with hot hide glue and a shopmade veneer hammer (see the photos on p. 24). Brush a thin coat of glue on the drawer front and on both sides of the veneer. Place the two pieces together and push a veneer hammer from the center in all directions to remove any air and excess glue. The hide glue hardens by cooling, so the process takes mere minutes. Use the shooting board to joint the veneer flush with the top and bottom. Trim the ends with a veneer saw. This is a special curved

saw with no set that allows you to cut veneer end grain flush with an edge.

Holding the drawer front in a vise, plane and scrape the veneer so it is smooth and uniform in thickness (see the photo on p. 25). Glue up the drawer, and while clamping, check for square. When it is dry, test the drawer's fit.

With a marking gauge, scribe the thickness of the cock beading on the ends of the drawer front and scribe its width on the dovetails. Cut this rabbet with a very sharp backsaw and clean it up with a shoulder plane. To avoid chipping the veneer, plane both edges toward the center.

Cut the top and bottom strips of cock beading to the same length as the drawer front. Using the edge of the rabbet as a guide, mark the joint's stopped miter. Stand the cock beading in a small miter box held in the bench hook and cut the miter with a very fine backsaw. Hold the top and bottom cock beading in place with clamps while you miter the two end pieces. Test their fit. Round the inside edges with a block plane and glue all four pieces of beading in place. When the glue is dry, level the cock beading with a block plane, if necessary, then round the outside edge with a sanding block.

The drawer should fit in its opening so the veneer is flush with the legs and the cock beading stands proud. To do this, glue two small blocks of pine to the drawer back to act as stops. Use a block plane to trim these blocks until they hold the drawer at the desired depth. The final decision is the hardware. I used a period brass oval pull. However, a turned knob would also be appropriate.

MIKE DUNBAR is a contributing editor to *Fine Woodworking* magazine.

Sources

The Stanley Works
1000 Stanley Dr.
New Britain, CT 06053
800-225-5111
www.stanleyworks.com

Tilt-Top Table

BY MARIO RODRIGUEZ

As a woodworking instructor, I'm always looking for interesting and challenging projects to present in my classes. This Federal tilt-top tea table satisfies all of my criteria for an intermediate-level project: It's neat and compact with only a few parts, and the construction introduces students to both machine- and hand-tool techniques. The bonus is that the finished product is graceful in design and fits into almost any interior space.

In the 18th century, many of these small tables were made with local hardwoods, and there are a number of period examples in maple, walnut, and cherry. My version is made of mahogany, which is available from most commercial suppliers in the required thicknesses, from 4/4 to 12/4. I find mahogany ideal for the turning required in this project, and it takes a finish beautifully.

AN ELEGANT PROJECT builds hand- and machine-tool skills.

Begin by Turning the Column on the Lathe

The profile of the column is provided at half scale in the drawing on the facing page. The drawing can be enlarged 200% to full size on a copy machine and used as a pattern. Prepare the turning blank thick enough to accommodate a maximum diameter of roughly 2¾ in. I recommend using a solid piece, although gluing up two pieces is an option; however, you'll be left with a seam down the center of the column.

Prior to mounting the blank on the lathe, lop off the long corners on the bandsaw by either tilting the bandsaw table to 45° or holding the workpiece at 45° in a carriage. Once it's on the lathe, rough the blank into a cylinder with an even 2¾-in. diameter. Use a parting tool and your pattern to set up the diameters of all of the various elements on the turning.

Mahogany Tea Table

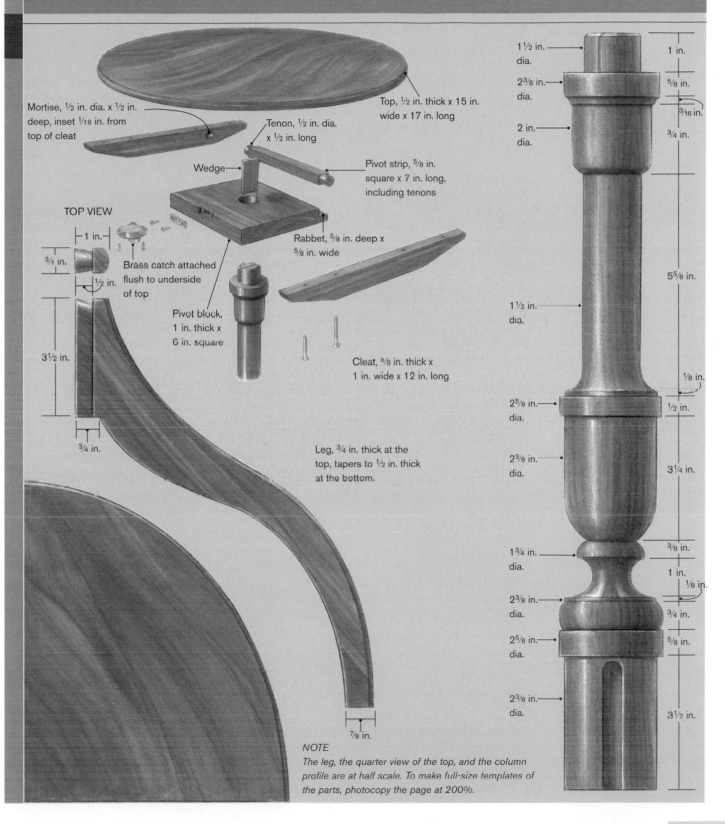

Mortise, ½ in. dia. x ½ in. deep, inset ¹/₁₆ in. from top of cleat

Top, ½ in. thick x 15 in. wide x 17 in. long

Tenon, ½ in. dia. x ½ in. long

Wedge

Pivot strip, ⁵/₈ in. square x 7 in. long, including tenons

TOP VIEW

1 in.

¾ in.

½ in.

3½ in.

¾ in.

Brass catch attached flush to underside of top

Pivot block, 1 in. thick x 6 in. square

Rabbet, ⁵/₈ in. deep x ⁵/₈ in. wide

Cleat, ⁵/₈ in. thick x 1 in. wide x 12 in. long

Leg, ¾ in. thick at the top, tapers to ½ in. thick at the bottom.

⁷/₈ in.

1½ in. dia.

2³/₈ in. dia.

2 in. dia.

1½ in. dia.

2⁵/₈ in. dia.

2³/₈ in. dia.

1¾ in. dia.

2³/₈ in. dia.

2⁵/₈ in. dia.

2³/₈ in. dia.

1 in.

⁵/₈ in.

³/₁₆ in.

¾ in.

5⁵/₈ in.

¹/₈ in.

½ in.

3¼ in.

³/₈ in.

1 in.

¹/₈ in.

¾ in.

⁵/₈ in.

3½ in.

NOTE

The leg, the quarter view of the top, and the column profile are at half scale. To make full-size templates of the parts, photocopy the page at 200%.

A Jig for Routing the Column

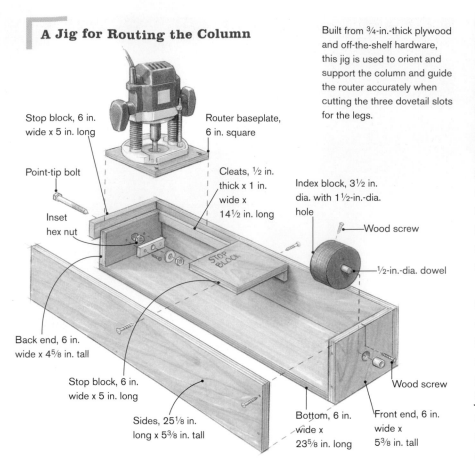

Built from ¾-in.-thick plywood and off-the-shelf hardware, this jig is used to orient and support the column and guide the router accurately when cutting the three dovetail slots for the legs.

Stop block, 6 in. wide x 5 in. long

Router baseplate, 6 in. square

Point-tip bolt

Inset hex nut

Cleats, ½ in. thick x 1 in. wide x 14½ in. long

Index block, 3½ in. dia. with 1½-in.-dia. hole

Wood screw

½-in.-dia. dowel

STOP BLOCK

Back end, 6 in. wide x 4⅝ in. tall

Stop block, 6 in. wide x 5 in. long

Sides, 25⅛ in. long x 5⅜ in. tall

Bottom, 6 in. wide x 23⅝ in. long

Front end, 6 in. wide x 5⅜ in. tall

Wood screw

Establish all of the flats first, then turn the coves and beads with a spindle gouge and a skew chisel. Finally, sand it smooth.

Turn column ends precisely Two critical portions of the column require careful attention. The diameter of the tenon at the top of the column, which engages the pivot block, must exactly match the 1½-in.-dia. hole drilled through the pivot block. Because I make this table so often in my classes, I made a plywood gauge that gives me the right diameter. However, you can just as well use a set of calipers.

The other critical area is the bottom portion of the column where the legs are attached. This end doesn't have to be turned to a precise diameter; just make sure it's straight and uniform. Any dips or a taper will create gaps where the column receives

the three dovetailed legs. A nonuniform surface also will have a detrimental effect on the fit of the legs.

Make a Carriage for the Sliding Dovetails

The traditional and most effective method of joining the legs to the column is with sliding dovetails. Once the legs have been attached, the flair of the dovetails prevents the legs from loosening over time. The key to achieving snug and handsome joints is to cut the slots first and then make the dovetails to fit.

To cut the joinery, you'll have to remove the turning from the lathe. Set up each cut carefully. I built a plywood carriage jig (see the drawing at left) that supports the column while I rout the dovetail slots. Each slot should be 120° apart on center, and the jig is equipped with an index block to align the column correctly for each slot. Match the 120° marks on the index block to a corresponding mark on the jig. A wood screw secures it in each position for cutting.

Cut the slots with three router bits There are three steps to cutting the dovetail slots. First, establish a flat edge on the column for the shoulder of the leg. Use a 1-in.-dia. straight router bit, and set up the cut to trim a flat surface just wide enough for the thickness of the leg. It's better to cut this a little too wide than too narrow. A wide flat can be rounded with a file, but a narrow flat will create a gap where the leg meets the column. The stop block on the router jig should be set so the dovetail slot stops just short of the column shoulder.

After cutting a flat edge for the three legs—rotating the column in the jig for each cut—switch to a ⁷⁄₁₆-in. straight bit and hog out most of the waste for each slot. This second step reduces the stress on the router and the wear on the dovetail bit. Finally, change router bits again to a dovetail bit (mine is an 11° bit) and take a final pass on each slot. Set the column aside until you're ready to cut the dovetails on the table legs.

Shape the Legs on the Bandsaw

The three legs are rough-cut on the bandsaw and taken to their final shape with hand tools. To begin, enlarge the scale drawing on p. 29 to 200% to make a template with ¼-in.-thick plywood, and then draw the leg shape directly onto the three workpieces with the grain running lengthwise. I made the pattern about 1 in. longer than is found on period examples of the table so that it could be built for a standard 29-in. height. However, to build a more accurate reproduction, you simply can cut off the extra inch from the foot without greatly affecting the appearance of the table.

Once each leg has been rough-cut to about ¹⁄₁₆ in. to the line, gang the legs together with a clamp and clean up the front and back edges with a spokeshave followed by a cabinet scraper. Clamping all three legs together makes it easier to keep the edges square, and it reduces tearout at the edges.

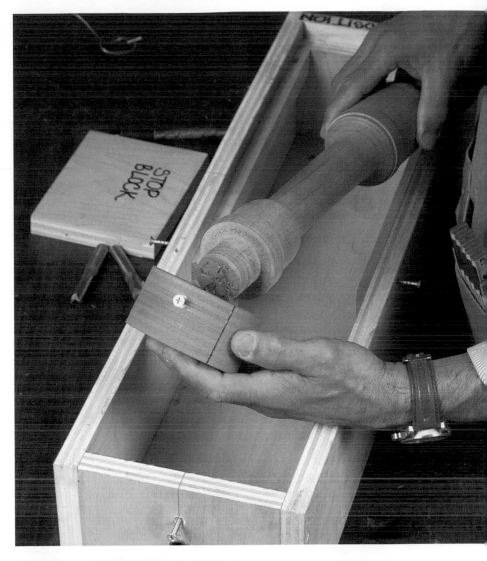

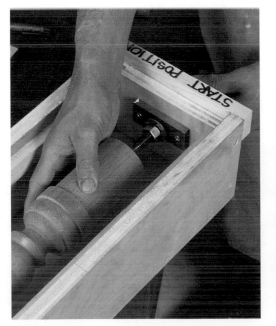

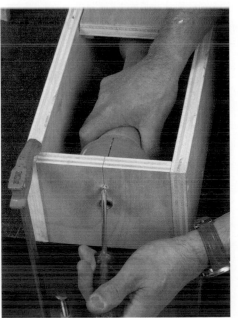

MOUNT THE COLUMN IN THE ROUTER JIG. First, insert the column into the index block and secure it with a wood screw to keep it from rotating within the block (above). Align the base of the column in the jig using the dimple created by the lathe and hold it in place by tightening the threaded rod (far left). Finally, locate the column for routing by aligning one of the three scribe lines on the index block with the centerline on the jig and fasten it with a screw (left).

Also, always cut in the direction of the grain with the spokeshave, even if it requires repositioning the legs in the vise.

Cut the Dovetails

To cut the dovetails on the legs, set up the router table with a fence and the same dovetail bit used for the slots. Before cutting into the real legs, use a cutoff from the leg material of the exact same thickness to make test cuts to fine-tune the fit of the dovetail into the column base. Carefully pass the stock upright along the fence to cut one cheek of the dovetail. Flip it over to cut the other side. I made a jig using my leg template that rides along the router-table fence and holds the leg steady. If you discover that a dovetail doesn't fit right in the column, run it back across the bit and apply more pressure against the fence. It might take off just enough to make the fit easier.

Next, make a slight roundover along the front edge of each leg one at a time. Draw a pencil line down the center of the leg as well as lines on both sides that follow the profile of the leg about ⅛ in. from the edge. Then use a spokeshave to round over the edge to your guide lines. Finish off to a nice profile with files, a scraper, and sandpaper.

Taper the legs The three legs taper from ¾ in. thick at the dovetail to ½ in. thick at the foot. I made a pair of sleds that help me create this taper with a thickness planer (see the top photos on p. 35), though careful handplaning also would work. The first sled elevates the foot of

Rout the Dovetail Slots in Three Steps

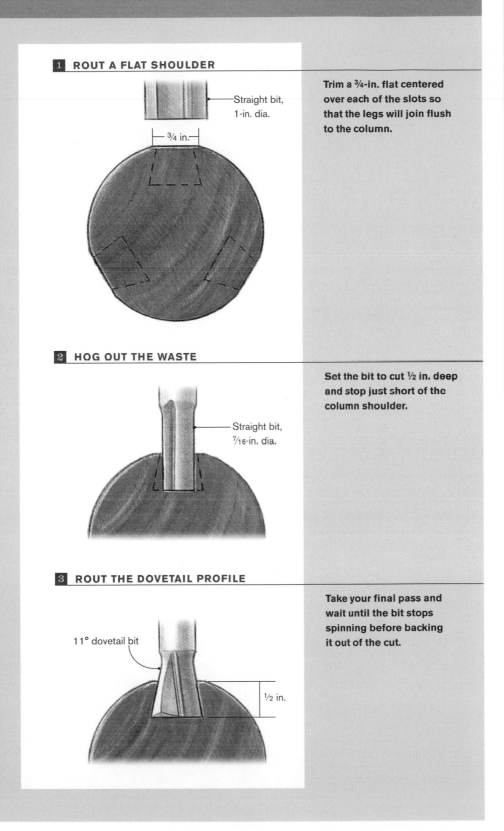

1 ROUT A FLAT SHOULDER

Straight bit, 1-in. dia.

¾ in.

Trim a ¾-in. flat centered over each of the slots so that the legs will join flush to the column.

2 HOG OUT THE WASTE

Straight bit, ⁷⁄₁₆-in. dia.

Set the bit to cut ½ in. deep and stop just short of the column shoulder.

3 ROUT THE DOVETAIL PROFILE

11° dovetail bit

½ in.

Take your final pass and wait until the bit stops spinning before backing it out of the cut.

Sources

For Behlen Solar-Lux stains:
Horton Brasses, Inc.
49 Nooks Hill Rd.
Cromwell, CT 06416
800-754-9127
www.horton-brasses.com

Garrett Wade Co., Inc.
161 Avenue of the
Americas
New York, NY 10013
800-566-9525
www.garrettwade.com

For installing a reproduction catch:
Whitechapel, Ltd.
P.O. Box 11719
Jackson, WY 83002
307-739-9478
www.whitechapel-ltd.com

Shape the Legs and Cut the Dovetails

SHAPE THE LEGS.
Gang the legs together with clamps and use a spokeshave and card scraper to clean up the bandsaw marks.

MAKE A JIG FOR ROUTING THE DOVETAILS. A jig, made using the leg template, supports the leg while routing. The sides of the jig ride on a supplemental fence screwed to the router-table fence. Put steady pressure against the fence as you rout to ensure a clean cut and tight fit.

the leg ⅛ in., creating one side of the taper when it is run through the planer. The second sled raises the foot of the leg ¼ in. so when you flip it over it cuts an even taper on both sides. Be careful not to plane off too much, or you will damage the dovetail.

Create the Tilting Mechanism

The pivot system for the tilting tabletop consists of a pivot block that fits over the column tenon and two cleats that attach to the underside of the tabletop. Two round tenons extend off one end of the pivot block and are set into holes in the two cleats, allowing the tabletop to pivot.

Make the two cleats and then drill the holes for the round tenons, locating them as close to the top edge as possible; I aim for about 1/16 in. This will ensure that the tabletop lies properly against the pivot block when it is horizontal and stands perfectly plumb when vertical.

There are two ways you can approach the pivot block. The traditional method is to cut the round tenons out of the pivot block with a single piece of wood. But the easiest method is to make a pivot block with a rabbet cut into one edge, and then glue in a separate strip sized to the dimensions of the rabbet with round tenons cut on each end. You will need to plane the pivot strip flush with the surface and the back edge of the pivot block.

Turn the round tenons on the lathe, and aim carefully for a squeaky-tight fit in the cleats. As the top is tilted, there should be some resistance on the pivot. That way, when the top is vertical, it will stay there.

Prepare the Oval Top

The tabletop measures about 15½ in. wide by 17½ in. long, so you may have to glue up two pieces to make it.

Using the scale drawing to make a ½-in.-thick birch plywood template, trace an outline of the tabletop onto the work-

ROUND THE FRONT EDGE OF THE LEGS. To guide your progress, mark the leg with a centerline and two guidelines along the sides about ⅛ in. from the edge.

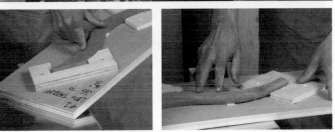

USE A PAIR OF SLEDS TO TAPER THE LEGS. Taper the legs with a thickness planer. Cut one side of the taper with a sled that raises the foot of the leg ⅛ in. Use a second sled to taper the other side. This time the foot is raised ¼ in. so that it is evenly tapered.

GLUE THE LEGS IN THE COLUMN. Apply glue liberally to each dovetail and tap it into the slot until it's fully set.

piece, and cut it out on the bandsaw just outside of the line. Next, rout the oval shape on a router table with a bearing-guided bit. The tabletop edges are slightly rounded over to match the rounded profile of the legs.

Assemble the Table, Apply a Finish, and Attach the Hardware

Once all of the parts have been prepared, assembly should go pretty smoothly. First, attach the legs to the column, checking for a tight fit and a clean joint between the

shoulder of the legs and the column. This should go on without incident if you carefully cut the dovetails on the router table. Although not required, you can reinforce the leg joints with a metal brace called a table spider—available from Horton Brasses (see "Sources" on p. 33).

Once the legs have been glued in place, use a wedge to attach the pivot block to the top of the column. Saw down the center of the column tenon to make a kerf for the wedge. It should run perpendicular to the direction of the grain on the pivot block so the block doesn't split when you drive

ALIGN THE BLOCK BEFORE SECURING IT. Align the pivot block on end while two legs are flat against the workbench. This will ensure that the legs are properly aligned with the oval top.

BUILD THE TILT MECHANSIM. Assemble the pivot block. Glue a separate strip with round tenoned ends into a rabbet cut in the pivot block. Then round the corner of the block to allow the table to tilt properly.

SCREW THE CLEATS TO THE TABLETOP. Slide the cleats onto the round tenons of the pivot block and center the base assembly along the long axis of the tabletop. Attach the catch after the finish has been applied.

A WEDGE SECURES THE PIVOT BLOCK. Orient the slot in the tenon perpendicular to the grain of the block to avoid splitting the block as you drive in the wedge.

home the wedge. The pivot block must be positioned so that when the tabletop is in the upright position, one leg is pointing straight back. This way the table can fit into a corner. To achieve the proper orientation, set the column onto a workbench so that two legs rest on the workbench (see the left photo on the facing page). Then attach the pivot block with the round tenons flat on the workbench.

Next, screw on the tabletop. With the top upside down on your workbench and the pivot block centered on it, set the cleats onto the pivot-block tenons with a ¹⁄₁₆-in. gap between. Then drive #8 screws through the cleats and into the underside of the tabletop.

All of the parts should be sanded through to 220-grit abrasive before

assembly. I stained the table with a mixture of cherry and walnut Behlen Solar-Lux™ stains (see "Sources"). Then I brushed on several thin coats of shellac. Sand lightly after the first coat of shellac and allow each subsequent coat to dry thoroughly. Finally, rub out the finish with fine steel wool.

The last step is to apply a glaze coat. I used McCloskey's glaze with raw umber Japan pigment added. Once the glaze dried, I waxed and buffed the table.

Finally, install a good reproduction catch (see "Sources") to keep the top secure and level when the table is in use.

MARIO RODRIGUEZ is a contributing editor to *Fine Woodworking* magazine.

Drop-Leaf Breakfast Table

BY ROBERT TREANOR

As an apartment dweller, I am constantly fighting a losing battle for space. In one small, narrow hallway in my apartment, the phone and its paraphernalia has to share space with one of the precious closets. Little room is left for a table on which to write messages or to place small items. It seemed to me that a drop-leaf table, narrow when closed, would fit the space and provide terms for a truce in my little battle. And as a peace dividend, I could always open up the table and use it elsewhere for special occasions.

The small table I made, as shown in the photo at left, is a good example of a late Queen Anne breakfast table. The 18th-century form combines grace and versatility, and making it demands the same attributes in the craftsman. The half-blind dovetailed aprons, the rule-jointed leaves, and the knuckle joints on the swing legs all require precise work. And shaping the compound curves of the cabriole legs needs a steady hand and eye. The skills are not difficult to master, and the effort will be rewarded with a useful and elegant table. The original on which my table is based was made of walnut, but I built mine of cherry. Maple or mahogany would also be appropriate. I used pine for the small amount of secondary wood.

MODESTY AND MAJESTY. This small Queen Anne breakfast table contains a broad range of joinery. Pinned tenons, knuckle joints and half-blind dovetails connect the aprons and legs, and rule joints run between the leaves and fixed top.

Drop-Leaf Table

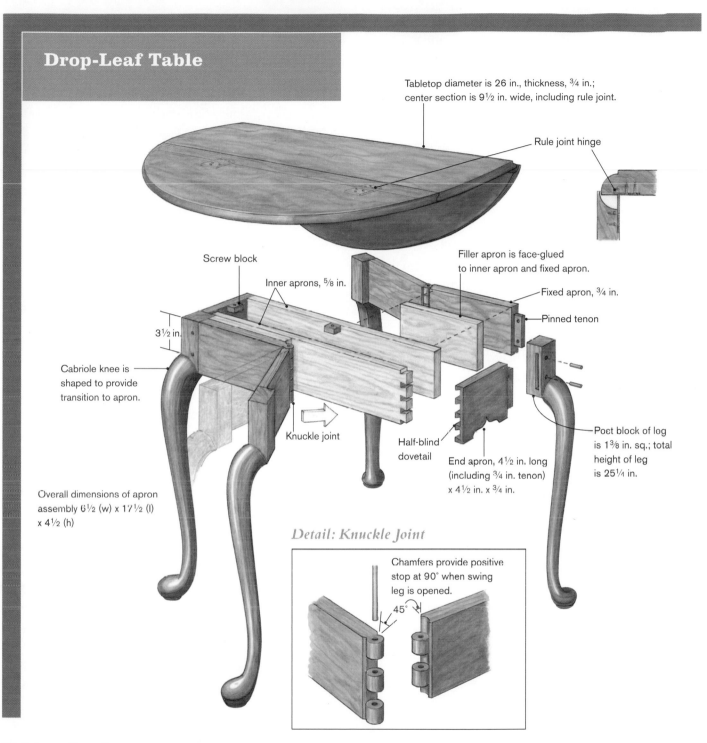

Tabletop diameter is 26 in., thickness, ¾ in.; center section is 9½ in. wide, including rule joint.

Rule joint hinge

Screw block

Inner aprons, ⅝ in.

Filler apron is face-glued to inner apron and fixed apron.

Fixed apron, ¾ in.

Pinned tenon

3½ in.

Cabriole knee is shaped to provide transition to apron.

Knuckle joint

Half-blind dovetail

End apron, 4½ in. long (including ¾ in. tenon) x 4½ in. x ¾ in.

Post block of log is 1⅜ in. sq.; total height of leg is 25¼ in.

Overall dimensions of apron assembly 6½ (w) x 17½ (l) x 4½ (h)

Detail: Knuckle Joint

Chamfers provide positive stop at 90° when swing leg is opened.

45°

Taking Stock

Begin the table by milling the required material. Leave the leg billets slightly over-size, and set them aside for a few days so any movement can later be planed out. The pieces that will form the side aprons should be left a few inches over finished length at this point. The extra length will allow you

to recut the knuckle joint for the hinge of the swing leg if necessary. Cut the fixed top and the leaves from the same board, so color and figure will be consistent.

Knuckle Joint Is Linchpin

The knuckle joints are at the heart of the table, and I start with them. The joint and the aprons it connects must be accurately aligned to ensure the fly leg stands vertically both in its home position, where it must meet the end apron squarely, and in its open position, where it must support the leaf at just the height of the fixed top.

A knuckle joint is basically a finger joint with its fingers rounded over and the bottoms of its sockets coved. To provide a positive stop for the swing leg at 90°, the joint has mating 45° chamfers on both aprons, as shown in the drawing detail on p. 39. The knuckles can be cut on the tablesaw with a finger-joint jig and then finished with hand tools. With only two joints to cut, though, I opted to make the entire joint with hand tools.

Cutting and fitting the joint is not difficult, but accurate layout is essential to success. Begin the layout by marking in from the end of each piece by the thickness of the material. Then carry a line around the apron at that point. Draw diagonal lines in the square you've created on the top and bottom edges of the stock, and draw a circle, as shown in the left photo below.

The short section of the diagonals between the circle and the original layout line is the chamfer line. To make chamfering easier and more accurate, you'll need

a relief cut. Draw a line parallel to the first layout line, and score along it with the corner of a sharp chisel guided by a square. Then chisel a shallow V-groove on the side of the line nearest the end of the board. The groove provides a channel for your saw to ride in as you start the relief cut. Make the relief cut with a tenon saw or dovetail saw, stopping just as the kerf touches the circle laid out on the edge of the board. Now make a guide block beveled at 45°, and ride a rabbet plane on the bevel to cut the chamfers, as shown in the right photo below.

Shape the barrels of the hinge with chisels and a block plane. Refer to the circles on each edge of the board as you proceed. Begin the rounding by planing a series of facets from end to end. Continue cutting narrower facets until the barrel is round. You could also use a router for some of the rounding over. A piece of scrapwood can be coved to the same radius as the barrel and used as a sanding block for final smoothing.

Lay out and cut the sockets between the knuckles next. Divide the board into five equal units across its width, and extend the division lines around the barrels. Using a backsaw, cut down the waste side of the

LAY OUT THE KNUCKLE JOINTS ACCURATELY, and you're halfway to a good hinge. The diagonals determine the hinge center point.

RUN A RABBET PLANE ALONG A GUIDE BLOCK to cut the chamfer that limits the swing of the knuckle joint hinge.

SCOOP OUT THE CENTER SOCKETS WITH A STRAIGHT CHISEL. Cove the outside sockets with a gouge of appropriate radius.

BILLET REBUILT. With the blade guide lowered to just above the stock, bandsaw along the layout lines. Tape the cabriole cutoffs back in place, and turn the billet 90° to make the second pair of cuts. After turning the foot, clean up the bandsawn curves with a spokeshave.

lines to the chamfer, and then chop out the waste material with a chisel, as you would when cutting dovetails, working from both sides to avoid chipout.

The bottoms of the sockets must be coved so they mate with the radius of the knuckles. Use gouges that match the sweep of the cope for the end sockets and a straight chisel to shape between the knuckles, as shown in the left photo above.

I used a piece of ³⁄₁₆-in. drill rod for the hinge pin. A length of brazing rod or dowel rod would also work. To drill the hole, assemble the joint on a flat surface and clamp it together end to end with a pipe clamp. Then clamp the whole assembly to a fence on the drill-press table, and drill the hole. To avoid bit wander, drill a little more than halfway through the joint, then flip the assembly and complete the hole from the opposite edge.

Drive the hinge pin into the joint, and check the action of the hinge. It should move smoothly without binding or much squeaking. When the joint is open to 90°, the two chamfers should form a gapless line. Set the aprons on a flat surface to ensure that they sit perfectly flat both when in line and at 90°.

Joining Legs and Aprons

It is best to cut the leg-to-apron mortise-and-tenon joints before shaping the legs. With the legs square, the whole process is easier and more accurate. The fly legs each have one mortise and the fixed legs have two. I cut the mortises with a plunge router, holding the legs in a simple box on which I guide the router. You could also chop them by hand or with a hollow-chisel mortiser. I find it quick and efficient to cut the tenons with a dado head on the tablesaw. For these tenons, which are ¾ in. long, I stacked the dado set ¾ in. wide and made the whole cut in one pass.

The end aprons have a tenon cut on one end and a half-blind dovetail on the other. Start the dovetailing by laying out and cutting the tails on the pine inner apron. Then use the tails to lay out the pins on the end apron. Before putting the end aprons aside, cut the ogee detail on their bottom edge.

Cabriole Curves Emerge

Named after the French dancing term for a leap, cabriole legs do give furniture a certain vitality or spring. And they're not all that difficult to make. A small portion of the

SHAPING THE FOOT. Only the lower part of the foot and the pad are shaped on the lathe. To provide good purchase for the live center, leave the leg full-sized above the knee until after turning.

work is done on the lathe—the foot and the pad beneath it. The rest of the shaping is done with the bandsaw and hand tools.

The leg blanks have been milled square and mortised by now. Leave the horn at the top (the extra inch that reduces the risk of a split during mortising) to provide waste for chucking on the lathe. Make a full-sized template of the leg out of thin plywood or poster board, and use it to lay out the cabriole curves on the two adjacent inside surfaces of the leg. Then cut out the legs on the bandsaw. Cut the curves only; don't cut out the post block (the section above the knee) until you've turned the feet. If you were to cut away the post-block waste now, it would be difficult to center the leg blank on the lathe. When you've cut one curve, tape the cutoff back into place, and cut the second face (see the top right photo on p. 41).

Untape the cutoff, and mount the leg between centers on the lathe. Then turn the major diameter of the foot. Measure up from the bottom ¼ in., and use a parting tool to establish the pad of the foot. With the major and minor diameters defined, use a small gouge or a scraper to shape the foot's profile, as shown in the photo above. Finally, before removing the leg from the lathe, sand the foot. Then you can take the legs to the bandsaw and cut away the waste above the knee.

The remainder of the leg shaping is done at the bench with an assortment of hand tools. You can hold the leg with a bar clamp clamped in your bench vise. The first step is to fair the bandsawn curves with a spokeshave. Be particularly careful working at the top of the foot because this is end grain and will chip easily. The front arris of the leg, though it moves in and out, should be a straight line when seen from the front.

Once the spokeshave work is complete, use a cabinetmaker's rasp to cut chamfers on the corners of the leg. Leave the corners sharp in the area above the knee. Next use the rasp to round over the chamfers and blend the curves of the leg, as shown in the photo on the facing page. The cross-section of the leg should be circular at the ankle and square with rounded corners just below the knee. When you've finished the coarse shaping with the rasp, refine the curves with a file. Further smoothing can be done with a hand scraper and sandpaper.

Next, shape the knee to provide a transition between the leg and apron, as shown in the drawing on p. 39. Lay out a curved line from the top of the knee to the point where the apron joins the leg. Then cut away the waste above the line with a sharp bench chisel. With the same chisel, shape the knee in a smooth curve. Once the shaping of the legs and knees is complete, saw the horns from the legs. Give all the parts a final sanding, and you are ready to glue up the table base.

Assembly and Subassembly

With 10 separate pieces composing its apron, this table presents an unusual challenge in the gluing up. The way I do it, there are three stages. First glue up the half-blind dovetail joints that link the end aprons to the inner aprons. Make sure the aprons meet at exactly 90° before setting them aside to dry. Next glue one fixed and one swing leg to each of the hinged aprons. A bar clamp with pads on the jaws will work well. To keep the hinge from pivoting, use handscrew clamps with light pressure to clamp the hinge to the bar clamp. Set all four subassemblies aside to dry overnight.

To complete the base assembly, you'll need two filler aprons made from secondary wood. They are face-glued between the fixed section of the hinged apron and the inner apron (see the drawing on p. 39). The fit has to be perfect, so dry-assemble the subassemblies, measure the gap, and mill the filler apron at that point. Glue the filler apron between the inner and outer aprons, keeping all three aligned with brads or biscuit joints.

The final glue-up is best done with the base upside down on a flat table. While the pieces are dry-clamped, check that the hinge will open through its range unimpeded. Then glue up the last two apron-to-leg joints. After the glue-up, pin all the mortise-and-tenon joints with ¼-in.-dia. pegs.

Rule Joints

I cut the rule joints that connect the leaves and the fixed top before roughing out the circular shape of the top. I do mill the boards carefully, though, and scrape or plane off the millmarks before cutting the rule joint. I find it easiest to cut the joint on a router table. First, cut the roundover on the fixed top with a ½-in. roundover bit. Guide

SHAPE AND BLEND THE CURVES of the cabriole legs with rasps and files. The leg should be round at the ankle and square with rounded corners just below the knee.

the top against a fence, and make trial cuts on scrapwood. Leave a ⅛-in. fillet at the top of the cut. Then chuck up a ½-in. core-box bit, and cut the leaves to fit the fixed top.

When installing the rule-joint hinges, leave some leeway for the top to expand and contract with variations in humidity. Instead of aiming for a joint that will close entirely on top, offset the hinge barrels ¹⁄₆₄ in. to ¹⁄₃₂ in. toward the leaf.

Once the hinges are in, lay out the top's diameter on its underside. It can be cut out by hand or with a bandsaw or a sabersaw. Scrape and sand the edge to remove the sawmarks, and shape the edge to a slight belly with planes, files, and sandpaper. Give the top a final sanding, and attach the base to it with screws driven through slotted holes in screw blocks attached to the inner aprons.

I finished the table with several coats of a tung oil/Danish oil mix. A coat of paste wax was applied after the oil finish was completely dry. Make sure the underside of the top and the inside surfaces of the aprons receive the same amount of finish as the visible surfaces. If you skimp on finish underneath, the table will take on and lose moisture unevenly and could be prone to warping.

ROBERT TREANOR, a former teacher in the woodworking program at San Francisco State University, builds and writes about furniture in the Bay area.

Construct a Classic Bed

BY DOUG MOOBERRY
AND STEVE LATTA

We build four-poster bed frames using the same basic construction that has held together for more than 200 years: Mortise-and-tenon joinery connects the head and foot rails to the posts; both side- and end-rail tenons are held in their post mortises by bed bolts and nuts. This lets us easily assemble and knock down the frame, and it allows us to tighten up the joints when the wood moves. To improve the traditional construction methods, we use modern tools and production techniques when shaping components and cutting joinery. And unlike a conventional bed frame that supports the mattress on a box spring, we prefer a different mattress-suspension system, which eliminates the box spring and allows us greater design opportunities (see the photo at left).

We came up with a way to support a mattress on a sheet of melamine, which rests on slats (see the drawing on p. 46). Then we can downsize the rails because they no longer have to cover a box spring (see the left photo on the facing page). This construction, called a platform bed, permits the rails to be located higher on the post, which enables more shaping of the leg section. Having higher rails also makes it easier to clean under the bed, and you're less likely to knock your shins when you get into the bed. While discussing the frame design we use, including how we allow for headboard wood movement, we'll describe the setups we use to simplify and speed up the bed-building process in our shop.

TRADITIONAL DETAILS SUIT A MODERN BED DESIGN. The simple shapes and light component sizes of this bed's cherry frame allow it to be easily situated in any bedroom. Whether the size is king, queen, full, or twin (as shown here), the authors prefer this same basic box-spring-less construction. A sheet of ¾-in. melamine, resting on slats, supports the bed's mattress.

Bed Design

Before we mill any wood for a bed, we completely work up the design with the customer, offering historical research when necessary. It's important that the post style and headboard shape complement the existing furniture of a bedroom (see the photo on the facing page). To get traditional ideas, we often look in antique magazines, museums, and Wallace Nutting's *Furniture Treasury* (see "Sources" on p. 50). For contemporary ideas, we look at old *Design Books* (The Taunton Press) or in back issues of *Architectural Digest*. We never just reproduce a bed, though. By refining proportions, using unusually figured wood, or choosing a special finish, we can significantly improve a bed's appearance.

We encourage customers to order platform beds (those without box springs). There are other reasons to eliminate the box spring besides the disadvantages previously mentioned. First, box springs cost money. Second, you may need to hang a ruffle to disguise the box spring or to make the bedspread look right (a frame without a box spring allows you to extend the mattress over the rails, so the covers hang nicely). Third, box springs make moving a challenge. Just ask any mover who has confronted a curved stairway with a queen-size bed.

Our platform beds get their influence from early 18th-century beds. This style remained popular up through the late 1700s. At that time, Thomas Sheraton developed "field beds," which were used in military tents because the frames could be easily disassembled and relocated. Aside from their ability to knock down, the best feature of a bolt-together bed is its versatility. By swapping different post styles (see the right photo above), we've made everything from traditional canopy beds to contemporary low-post beds—in sizes from twin to king. (Refer to the chart on p. 47 for overall

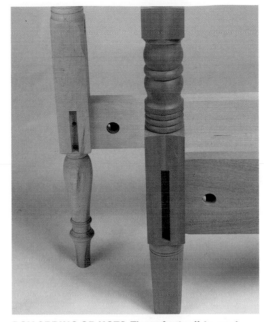

BOX SPRING OR NOT? These foot rail-to-post assemblies are similar. However, the mahogany frame (right) requires a box spring, while the maple frame (left) does not. Because the left assembly's rails do not have to cover a box spring, they can be narrower and located higher on the post, which allows better shaping of the leg.

frame and component dimensions based on typical mattress sizes.)

Stock Preparation

After we've arrived at a bed's size and style, the next step is to measure the mattress exactly. We once built a bed from dimensions that were given to us by a mattress salesman. Because he gave us the wrong height, we wound up with a bed whose headboard barely showed above the pillows. Now we always measure the mattress twice, and we usually yell at the salesman once. This is also the time we order the bed hardware, such as bed bolts and their covers (available from Ball & Ball or Horton Brasses Inc., see "Sources").

Depending on what a customer prefers, we usually select bed-frame stock from wood stored in our barn. We use common hardwoods like cherry, maple, walnut, and mahogany. Generally, we allow thick green wood to dry a year to reach about

YOU CAN CREATE A WIDE RANGE OF TURNED or shaped bedposts. Here are a sampling of post sizes and styles in cherry. From the left: New England traditional (yet to be finished), country Sheraton, fluted Chippendale, pencil post, and contemporary (with a bed-bolt hole showing).

Detail A: Double Mortise in Head Post

Notch 3/8 in. at top.

Headboard

Notch is 3/8 in. below face of post.

Leave wood to stiffen center of mortise.

Gaps, 1/8 in., allow headboard expansion.

Post

Detail B: Split Tenon on Headboard

Post

Upper tenon fits snugly.

Headboard

Lower tenon floats.

Gaps, 1/8 in., allow headboard expansion.

Detail C: Rail-to-Post Bed Bolt

Post

Hole, 1 in. dia. x 3/4 in. deep

Mortise, 13/16 x 3/4 x 4 1/2

Gap, 1/8 in.

Hole, 3/8 in. dia.

Rail

Gap, 1/16 in.

2 1/4 in.

Hole, 1 1/4 in. dia. x 1 1/2 in. deep

Centerline

Head post

Headboard

DETAIL B

DETAIL A

Head rail

Slat bracket
1/4 in. x 3 in. x 3 in.

Slats, 2x4, on edge for king-, queen-, and full-size beds

Height of side rail depends on desired mattress location.

Foot post

Z

Y

Cope to fit post.

Melamine, 3/4 in., supports mattress.

Side rail

Note: Dimensions X, Y, Z, L, and W depend on mattress size. See the chart on p. 47 for information.

Ledge strip, 1x1, screwed to rail

Slats, 2x4, laid flat for twin-sized bed

DETAIL C

L

W

X

Bed-bolt cover

Foot rail

Hole, 1 1/4 in. dia. x 1 1/2 in. deep, on inside of rail, captures bed-bolt nut.

13% moisture content before we kiln-dry it. We make sure that all four bedposts come from the same log (glued-up posts are unacceptable in our shop). In addition, we carefully match the headboard stock to the posts, and we try to select rail stock that is similar in grain and color to the posts. Next, we rough-cut the stock, allowing extra length for rail tenons and for parting off posts if they're to be turned. Then we let the stock sit in the shop a while before we mill it.

Frame Construction

The mattress-suspension system we use begins with 2x4 slats; three laid on their side for a twin bed, four laid on edge for a double or queen, and five on edge for a king-size bed. To hold up the slats on a twin frame, we screw a ledger strip around the interior of the rails (see the drawing on the facing page). For larger beds, we install slat-hanging brackets (angle iron) above the bottom of the rail. On top of the base of slats, we lay a sheet of ¾-in. melamine. The melamine stiffens and squares the frame, supports the mattress, and, because it is smooth, prevents the mattress cover from tearing. We screw the slats to the brackets so that the top of the melamine lies at or just below the top of the rails.

Posts Each post has three sections: the leg, the block, and the top. The leg likes to be at least 14 in. long to allow for proper shaping (see the left photo on p. 45) and to strengthen the rail connection by reducing the lever arm of the upper post. The center block needs to be at least 1 in. longer than the rail height (longer if you want to shape transitional lamb's tongues). The block size should also look proportionate to the rest of the post (see the right photo on p. 45). The top section of the post carries the headboard and is the most visible area of the bed. To figure the length of the top of a head post, we place headboard and post

BED PROPORTIONS				
Mattress size ✳ (w x l)	**King** (76 x 80)	**Queen** (60 x 80)	**Full** (54 x 75)	**Twin** (39 x 75)
Length of side rails ◆	80½	80½	75½	75½
Length of head and foot rails ◆ ▶	73½	56½	50½	37
Head-post height (Y) ✖				
Top	24	22	20	17
Block	6	6	6	5
Leg	14	14	14	14
Foot-post height (X) ✖				
Top	9	9	9	9
Block	6	6	6	5
Leg	14	14	14	14
Post section (square) ✖	2¾ to 3½	2¾ to 3½	2¾ to 3½	2¾ to 3½
Rail section (W x L) ✖	5 x 1¾	5 x 1¾	5 x 1¾	4 x 1¾
Headboard width (Z) ✖	20	18	16	13

Notes:
◆ Length of rails includes tenons.
✳ Frames shown require no box spring. Mattress sizes shown are industry standards.
✖ Post, rail, and headboard sizes are for traditional bed (see photo on p. 44).
▶ Add two rail thicknesses to frame width if you want mattress inset from rails.

patterns against the stock to make sure the connection will occur at a sensible place. To figure the length of foot posts, we mark the posts a couple of inches above where the mattress top will be.

We send 90% of our bed posts to local turner Mark Taylor to do the shaping. Along with stock for the posts, we give him a full-scale pattern showing the spindle design. Once the posts have been shaped, we determine the rail height. Then we lay out the center of the mortises on the correct faces of the post. We extend a bottom line around all the faces to use as a reference line for drilling bed-bolt holes later (see drawing detail on the facing page).

To waste the bed-post mortises, you can use a plunge router and the jig shown in

ROUTING BED-POST MORTISES. With a post wedged in this jig, you can easily rout mortises for the rail tenons whether the post is turned or shaped. Then, just use a chisel to square the mortises' corners. For adjustability, the router base slides in tracks in the carriage, and one of the jig's rails has slots for its mounting screws.

SAWING BED-RAIL TENONS. A 10-in. dado set in the radial-arm saw makes quick work of tenons. To ensure proper registration on bowed rail stock, the authors screwed a spacer block to the left fence (with clearance for the guard), and they shaped the right stop so that it contacts the center of the tenon end.

the top left photo. The jig is easy to construct and is adjustable to fit most posts. We made our jig's base out of particleboard and poplar, and we capped the rails with hardwood runners. We screwed together plywood and scraps to make the router carriage. If a post is tapered, we insert a couple of shims before clamping it between the jig's rails. Next, we double-check each mortise layout because the post is scrap if the location is wrong. Then, using a ½-in., two-spiral end mill (Forest City Tool Co., see "Sources"), we rout one side of the mortise, rotate the setup 180°, and rout the other side. Although the bit leaves rounded ends, it's quick and easy to square the mortises with a hand chisel.

Rails After we dimension the rails, we cut their tenons on a radial-arm saw fitted with a 10-in. dado head. To prevent transferring inaccuracies from slightly bowed or twisted stock, we space out the work from the saw's fence, and we butt the end of the rail against a pointed stop (see the bottom left photo). The stop contacts the same (center) spot on the rail when we flip it to cut the other cheek. To ensure a snug fit in the mortises, we cut the tenons thick, and we shave them down with a rabbet plane. After we have cleaned up the shoulders, we set the rail on edge, raise the sawblade, and then notch ⅝ in. on the top (but not the bottom) of the tenon. The notch allows the rail to expand and contract without exposing the post mortise. This orientation also helps us to tell which side of the rail is up during assembly (see drawing detail C on p. 46)

Headboard Because headboards are wide, lots of wood movement will occur. Cutting a long mortise to accept a slightly under-width tenon will handle the problem, but it's likely that the mortise will open up and leave an unsightly gap where the headboard meets the post. Therefore, we

BORING BED-BOLT HOLES. Steve Latta drills through a post into the end of a rail. The post hole is counter-bored for the bed-bolt head.

allow for expansion and contraction at the (cross grain) post-to-headboard joints by doing one of two things: We either shape a double mortise (leaving a center section of wood to stiffen the mortise) and notch the headboard ends to form twin tenons (see drawing detail A on p. 46), or we split the tenons on the headboard and undersize the lower tenons, so they float in their post mortises (as shown in drawing detail B on p. 46).

With split-tenon headboards, we lay out the tenons so that the lower one falls onto a flat, and the upper (snug) tenon falls just under a bead or other detail. Tapering the 13/16-in. headboard thickness on the tenons ensures that they'll fit tightly into the 3/4-in.-wide post mortises. We cope both the top and bottom of the lower tenons, so the mortises will be covered no matter which way the wood moves. If we use a double mortise, we undersize both of the tenons, notch the top of the headboard, and cope the shoulder to fit the post. This enables the wood to move without being seen.

To form the shape of a headboard, we make a full-scale template out of MDF. Each template, which we keep, is half of a headboard: We trace the left side, and then flip it to get the right side. This lets us fudge the length of a headboard, such as for larger bed frames. After we score the shape on the stock with an X-Acto® knife, we sabersaw close to the line. Then we clamp the pattern to the stock and flush-trim the shape using a bearing-guided router bit. To prevent tearout, we always rout down the headboard's slope.

Bed bolts Because we use authentic bed bolts in our frames, we provide the customer with a traditional wrench when we deliver the bed. We lay out the bed-bolt holes so the bolts will clear each other inside the post. A 1/2-in. offset spacing works well because this lets us hang adjacent bed-bolt covers at the same height. Boring the holes is a three-step process: First, we bore a hole in the post to recess the bolt head. The hole is large enough to fit the bed-bolt wrench, but small enough to be hidden

Sources

Wallace Nutting Library
www.wallacenuttinglibrary.com

Ball and Ball
463 W. Lincoln Hwy.
Exton, PA 19341
800-254-3711
www.ballandball-us.com

Horton Brasses
49 Nooks Hill Rd.
Cromwell, CT 06416
800-754-9127
www.horton-brasses.com

Forest City Tooling
Wood Tech Enterprises
P.O. Box 2226
Fairview, NC 28730
704-322-4266
www.forestcitytooling.com

by a bed-bolt cover. Second, we bore a 1½-in.-deep hole in the side of the rail (to house the nut), using a 1¼-in. Forstner bit chucked in our drill press. Having a rounded seat for the nut instead of a flat allows greater adjustment when it comes time to assemble the frame (see the photo below). And third, using the post hole as a guide, we center-bore a ⅜-in. hole (slightly larger than the bolt) through the post into the rail end using a 10-in.-long twist bit. To do this, we lay the post on its side, fit the tenon in its mortise, mark the mating parts on the inside with a punch, and then bore the hole with a hand drill (see the photo on p. 49).

If the layout is accurate, the bit will emerge in the center of the nut hole. We continue drilling into the rail to provide enough depth for the entire bed bolt (see drawing detail C on p. 46).

We assemble the posts, headboard, and rails before we sand and finish the frame. Once on site, we loosely assemble the frame and install the melamine, which squares up the frame. Then we snug all the bed bolts and lay down the mattress.

DOUG MOOBERRY AND STEVE LATTA build beds and other furniture at Kinloch Woodworking in Unionville, Pennsylvania.

ASSEMBLING THE HEAD OF THE BED. After Latta loosely tightens the bed bolts between the head rail and posts, he checks the fit of the headboard.

Making a Sheraton Bed

BY PHILIP C. LOWE

Beds often are very simple, even if they look as complicated as the Sheraton bed in the photo on p. 52. The joinery isn't complicated, and there aren't many parts. In fact, once you've made the posts for this bed, the hard work is behind you. Think about the posts as different circular-shaped moldings stacked on top of one another. The posts can be made in one piece, as I do, or made in several pieces, which are glued together later. The posts also can be made without decora-

tive reeding, which cuts out many hours of work on the project and still results in a pleasing design.

I always make full-scale drawings for pieces that I'm about to make. For this bed, I have to draw only one of the posts, half the shape of the headboard, and the joinery detail for the rail-post connection. I use the drawing to make a story stick (a scrap of wood where dimensions and profiles are marked), so laying out the bed posts is both easy and accurate.

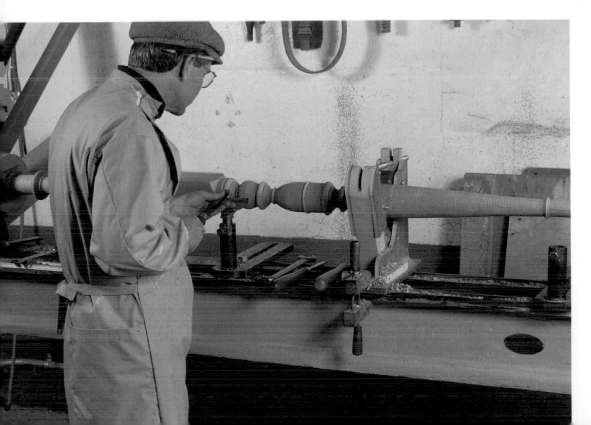

TURNED POSTS ARE THE MOST DRAMATIC FEATURE of a Sheraton bed. The posts can be turned in one piece, as the author did here, or turned in two or more pieces, which are glued together later.

A SHERATON-STYLE BED IS EASY TO MAKE, despite its complicated appearance. Reeding is time-consuming, but optional, and the joinery is straightforward. On this bed, the author skipped the reeding on the less-prominent headboard posts.

Mounting the Blank

The bedpost blanks are milled to 3½ in. sq. from 16/4 stock and rough cut to length, leaving a couple of inches at each end for mounting in the lathe. Turning the full-length blanks is no problem on my lathe, with its 10-ft.-long bed. But if you don't have this luxury, you will have to turn the post in sections and join them together by boring a hole in one part and turning a mating tenon on the adjoining member. The joints should be cemented with yellow glue or epoxied for extra strength. I've marked a few joining points, as shown in the drawing on the facing page. As a rule, the best place to join these parts is at a fillet above or below a cove, torus, or ogee shape.

I mount the blank at the headstock end with a faceplate and plywood disc drive center, which provides a more positive drive than a spur center. This arrangement also lets me add an indexing wheel (see the sidebar on p. 54) and makes it easy to remount the blank.

The drive center is a circular piece of ¾-in.-thick plywood screwed to the face-plate. The plywood has a square hole the size of the turning blank cut out of its center. To mount the blank, one end is slipped into the square hole, and the ball-bearing center in the tailstock is slid into position at the opposite end and locked in place.

Turning the Posts

The first step is to locate the post block, which is the nonturned section of the post into which the side and end rails are mortised. I scribe shoulder lines around the post, and with a backsaw, cut kerfs on all four corners at the shoulder points. The kerfs prevent the square edges of the post block from chipping when I turn the adjacent sections. After turning the post to the largest possible cylinder above and below the post block, I lay out and turn the pommels (the curved shoulders at the top and bottom of the post block).

To lay out the elements of the posts, I make up two story sticks or rods, one for the section above and one for the section below the post block. On the story sticks, I draw half the profile of the post and mark the diameter of each design element. I cut notches into the edge of the story stick with a skew chisel to make sure the pencil references are made from the same spot when each of the four posts is laid out.

I usually hold the story stick against the revolving blank to scribe the post. Another method is to mark the post with the story stick, as shown in the far left photo on the facing page. Then turn on the lathe, and hold the pencil point at the mark to extend the reference line completely around the post.

I shape the bottom of the post first, turning the cylindrical blank down to the diameters indicated on the story stick with a parting tool. I check each blank's diameter with calipers. Then I shape the curves and hollows with skews and gouges, leaving the cove or scotia cuts for last. Because the coves create the smallest diameters, leaving these cuts until the end helps to reduce vibration while turning the rest of the post.

The upper section of the post is turned in the same fashion, except I add a steady rest, as shown in the photo on p. 51, to help prevent the post from vibrating and being thrown out of round when turning. After I've turned this section to as accurate a cylinder as possible, I locate the steady rest at the bulbous section of the reeded portion of the post. With the steady rest in place, the upper section is turned to shape, again leaving the coves till last.

A SCRIBE LAYS OUT EVENLY SPACED REEDS. With a pencil set to the center of the lathe and its base riding on the lathe bed, a scribe accurately draws layout lines for reeds on the top of the bedposts.

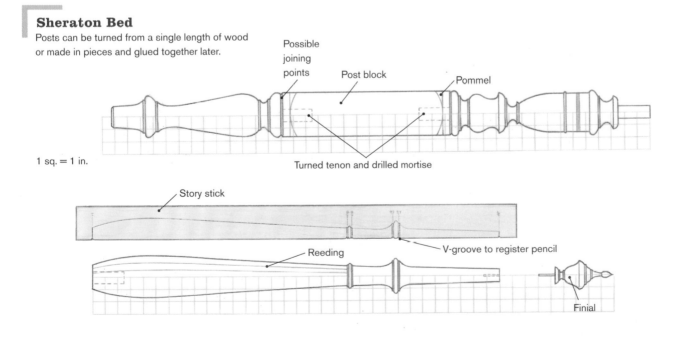

Sheraton Bed

Posts can be turned from a single length of wood or made in pieces and glued together later.

Possible joining points

Post block

Pommel

Turned tenon and drilled mortise

1 sq. = 1 in.

Story stick

Reeding

V-groove to register pencil

Finial

Indexing Wheels for the Lathe

The faceplate and plywood drive center that I use to turn my bedposts make the perfect mounting system for an indexing wheel. My indexing wheel is made by cutting a hole in the center of a 10-in.-sq. piece of ¼-in.-thick plywood. The hole fits the turning blank. After laying out the required number of divisions (16 for the bedposts) on the plywood with a compass, I bandsawed the plywood into a 10-in.-dia. circle. And I cut out the center square on the jigsaw.

Around the perimeter of the disk at each division line, I made a bandsaw cut 1 in. in from the edge of the disk. The indexing wheel is now ready to be slipped over the end of the post and then screwed to the faceplate and disk drive (see the photo at right).

The stop that engages the kerfs on the indexing wheel is simply a discarded piece of bandsaw blade with the teeth ground off. This stop is held even with the centerline of the lathe by an L-shaped plywood bracket, as shown in the drawing above.

To scribe lines or carve the reeding, I pivot the stop into a sawkerf to hold the post in position. To mark or carve the next and each consecutive line, I slide the stop back and rotate the post to the next sawkerf in the wheel. I slide the stop into place and scribe or carve the next division line.

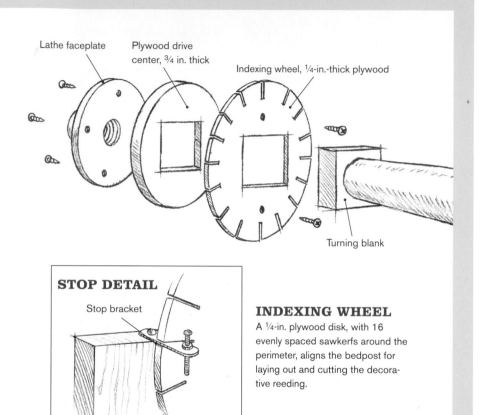

Lathe faceplate

Plywood drive center, ¾ in. thick

Indexing wheel, ¼-in.-thick plywood

Turning blank

STOP DETAIL

Stop bracket

INDEXING WHEEL

A ¼-in. plywood disk, with 16 evenly spaced sawkerfs around the perimeter, aligns the bedpost for laying out and cutting the decorative reeding.

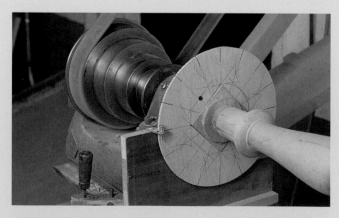

ACCURATE INDEXING FOR REEDING. A disk of ¼-in. plywood makes an indexing wheel for laying out reeding on the bedposts. The stop is a piece of bandsaw blade mounted even with the lathe center.

Once I've turned the posts to shape, I sand them, starting with 120 grit and working up to 220-grit. Between each sanding, I wet the post and let it dry to raise the grain. I sand everything but the section of post to be carved with reeds because the sanding grit would get in the pores of the wood and dull my carving tool.

Reeding the Posts

Because it takes about four hours to carve the reeds into each post, clients frequently choose to save money by eliminating the reeding entirely or by having just the posts of the footboard reeded, as shown in the photo at right on p. 52. Usually, these posts are prominently displayed near the middle of the room, and the headboard posts are generally pushed against a wall.

I've found the easiest way to lay out and carve the reeds is right on the lathe. To do this, though, you need an indexing wheel to hold the post in position for scribing the layout lines and carving the reeds. This is a standard feature on some lathes, but not mine, so I added one, as discussed in the sidebar on the facing page.

I also made a scribe for drawing the layout lines. The scribe rides on the lathe's bed and has a pencil set to the center height of the lathe. I mark one reed, as shown in the photo on p. 53, rotate the post, and mark another until the post is completely laid out. I use a V-carving tool to carve lines into the post and a series of straight and back-bent gouges to carve the reeds to their half-round shapes. When carving is complete, I sand the reeds.

Putting It All Together

After taking the post from the lathe, I drill a hole in the top of the post for a pin that will hold the finial in place and lay out and cut the mortises. There are two on each post block to accept the tenons for the rails and two more in each headboard post.

DRILLING HOLES FOR BED BOLTS. Holes bored through the bedposts serve as guides when drilling rails for the bed bolts. The nut is hidden in a mortise in the side of the rail.

The holes for the bed bolts are staggered, so the bolt for the end rail doesn't interfere with the bolt for the side rail. These ⅜-in.-dia. holes have a 1-in.-dia. counterbore to bury the head of the bolt. I bore the holes on the drill press, starting with the 1-in.-dia. counterbore and then the ⅜-in.-dia. bolt hole, aligning the bit with the center point of the counterbored hole.

I hand-drill the bolt holes into the ends of the rails, using the holes in the posts as a guide, as shown in the photo above. Mortises for the nuts are cut into the sides of the rails, so they intersect the bolt holes.

PHILIP C. LOWE designs, makes, and restores fine furniture in Beverly, Massachusetts.

Shaker-Style Clock

BY PHILIP C. LOWE

The simple beauty of Shaker styling teamed with modern clockworks offers an attractive and accurate timepiece as well as room for storage.

However, when I had a commission for such a Shaker clock, I found a lot of pictures of clocks, but no dimensioned drawings. So I scaled my design from a photo.

Because of my clients' space limitations, my version is only about 80% as large as the original. The dimensions of this downsized version fit very well in modern interiors. I proportioned the sides to the front, being careful to accommodate a modern quartz movement. That also left room for shelves in the lower compartment, which usually houses the pendulum.

The cherry and pine case is held together with typical Shaker construction: Mortises and wedged through-tenons join the carcase, and blind mortise-and-tenon joints connect the door frames.

THIS SHAKER-STYLE WALL CLOCK is a beautiful adaptation of the original design. Its smaller size, about 7 in. shorter than the original, fits well in modern homes, and the shelves added behind the panel door provide storage in a space that was intended for a pendulum.

Shaker-Style Wall Clock

Scaled from a photograph, this drawing shows the author's interpretation of a Shaker wall clock. Joinery is based on traditional Shaker construction techniques, but the size is about 20% smaller than the original clock, which was about 31 in. tall.

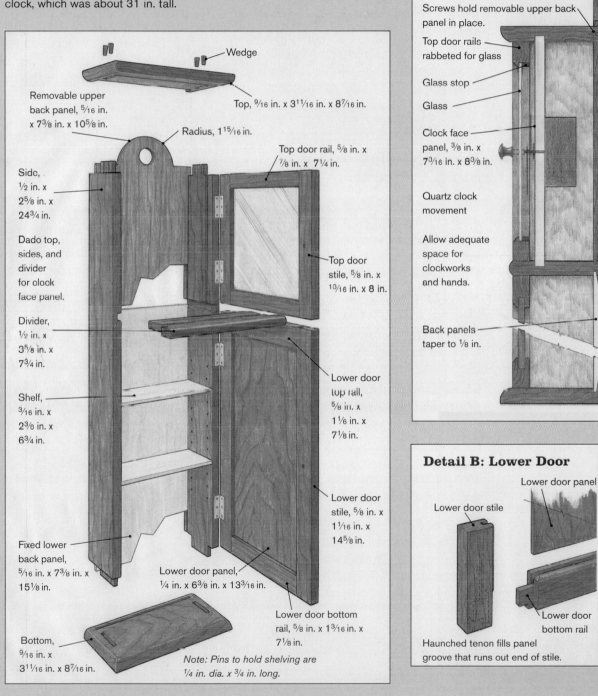

Wedge

Removable upper back panel, 5/16 in. x 7 3/8 in. x 10 5/8 in.

Top, 9/16 in. x 3 11/16 in. x 8 7/16 in.

Radius, 1 15/16 in.

Top door rail, 5/8 in. x 7/8 in. x 7 1/4 in.

Side, 1/2 in. x 2 5/8 in. x 24 3/4 in.

Dado top, sides, and divider for clock face panel.

Top door stile, 5/8 in. x 13/16 in. x 8 in.

Divider, 1/2 in. x 3 5/8 in. x 7 3/4 in.

Lower door top rail, 5/8 in. x 1 1/6 in. x 7 1/8 in.

Shelf, 3/16 in. x 2 3/8 in. x 6 3/4 in.

Lower door stile, 5/8 in. x 1 1/16 in. x 14 5/8 in.

Fixed lower back panel, 5/16 in. x 7 3/8 in. x 15 1/8 in.

Lower door panel, 1/4 in. x 6 3/8 in. x 13 3/16 in.

Lower door bottom rail, 5/8 in. x 1 3/16 in. x 7 1/8 in.

Bottom, 9/16 in. x 3 11/16 in. x 8 7/16 in.

Note: Pins to hold shelving are 1/4 in. dia. x 3/4 in. long.

Detail A: Top Door

Screws hold removable upper back panel in place.

Top door rails rabbeted for glass

Glass stop

Glass

Clock face panel, 3/8 in. x 7 9/16 in. x 8 9/16 in.

Quartz clock movement

Allow adequate space for clockworks and hands.

Back panels taper to 1/8 in.

Detail B: Lower Door

Lower door panel

Lower door stile

Lower door bottom rail

Haunched tenon fills panel groove that runs out end of stile.

Clock Design

A frequent admonition for any project is to buy your hardware before beginning to build. This is particularly true for a clock. You must accommodate hinges, latches, and clockworks, and don't forget to allow enough room between the clock's face and the glass in the door for the hands.

Although original Shaker clocks had wooden works, I substituted a quartz movement from Klockit, Inc. (see "Sources" on p. 60). Because the quartz movement I chose didn't have a pendulum, I added some shelves to the bottom compartment to make a convenient storage place for small items.

Hand-Detailed Stock Preparation

I use the normal array of woodshop machines, such as a jointer, planer, tablesaw, and crosscut saw, to dress and dimension stock slightly oversize for my projects. But to add a true, handcrafted touch and to remove machinery millmarks, I make a couple of light passes on each face and edge of the stock with a handplane. To cut pieces to length, I scribe my cutting line with a knife, rough-cut shy of the line on the tablesaw, and then handplane to the scribed line. I mold the edges of the top, bottom, and doors on a table-mounted router with the appropriate bit.

Planning Mortises and Tenons

When laying out the mortises and tenons for the carcase, I didn't want the grooves for the back to interfere with the sides' tenons. I was also worried that the ends of the top and bottom might split during assembly when I drove the wedges into the sides' tenons. I avoided both these prob-lems by extending the tenons' shoulders at the front and back and adding a shoulder to the outer side while leaving the inside barefaced, as shown in the drawing on p. 57. This way, the tenons clear the grooves, and the top and bottom mortises have greater strength.

Putting on a Good Face

The face and works fasten to a pine panel that sits in grooves cut in the sides, top, and divider. To ensure the face panel grooves line up, I referenced all the cuts off the back edges of these pieces. When cutting these grooves, be sure to allow clearance for the clock's hands.

Grooves for Double Back Panels

I used double panels in the back: a fixed lower panel and a removable upper panel for access to the clockworks. I beveled the back side of these 5/16-in.-thick panels, so their edges will fit into a 1/8-in.-wide groove.

The lower panel is captured in grooves in the sides, bottom, and divider. The grooves run from end to end on all pieces except the bottom, which has a stopped groove. Through-grooves are easily cut on the tablesaw, but a router is probably the safest way to cut the stopped groove.

The top back panel slides from the top into grooves in the sides and divider. The panel includes a semicircular section extending above the clock with a hole for hanging the clock on a Shaker peg. Two screws driven through the top panel and into the back edge of the top secure the removable back panel.

To let the back panel drop into its grooves, I use a tablesaw to cut away the back edge of the top, as shown in the draw-ing. I make this stopped cut by raising the

Reproducing an Aged Finish

Building accurate replicas of old pieces is always compromised when using new wood because it lacks the patina that develops only with age. This is particularly true of cherry, which darkens considerably as it ages. However, I've found a chemical solution that can impart an aged looked to cherry without waiting years.

I apply a saturated solution of Sal-Soda, an unpure carbonate of soda that painters use for cleaning prior to painting. Sal-Soda can be hard to track down, but you may find it at large, commercial paint-supply stores, or you can mail-order it from the Johnson Paint Co. (see "Sources"). One pound ($1.20/lb.) will make about 1½ gals. to 2 gals. of saturated solution.

I mix the Sal-Soda with water until no more crystals will dissolve, strain off the undissolved crystals, and then apply a heavy coat of the mixture with a foam brush. I wipe off any excess puddles of solution after approximately 15 minutes, let it dry thoroughly, and then apply a second coat. Because this process can raise the grain, it's important to wet-sand the piece several times before applying the Sal-Soda.

Sal-Soda also works on oak and mahogany, but it shouldn't be used on veneers. The solution must be neutralized with a vinegar and water wash before applying any topcoats. Results can vary, so experiment on scraps of the wood you're using, and allow about a week for the darkening to fully develop.

After treating with Sal-Soda, I brushed on three coats of orange shellac, allowing each coat to dry overnight and then rubbing between coats with 0000 steel wool. To add just a hint more color to the wood, I waxed the clock with a coat of Kiwi brown shoe polish and finished up with a clear coat of butcher's wax.

---

blade through the top with the same fence setting used to groove the sides, so the cut lines up with the grooves. Don't make this cut without a stop block clamped to the fence in front of the piece.

To position the stop block, I use the top, laid out with start and stop marks for the cut, as a gauge. I lay the marked top next to the blade and then raise the blade until the points at which the teeth of the blade penetrate the tablesaw top at the front and back of the blade are just shy of the start and stop marks on the top. I clamp the stop block to the fence and lower the blade, counting the number of turns until the blade is completely retracted. After positioning the top against the fence and the stop block, I turn on the saw and raise the blade through the stock, the same number of turns it took to lower it, being sure to keep my fingers clear of the cutting area. I then lower the blade, turn off the saw, and finish the cuts with a handsaw.

Although this procedure is easily done, you might be more comfortable just cutting away the waste on a bandsaw.

Assembly and Glue-Up

Before assembly, I drilled holes for the shelf pins in the sides and then sanded the carcase pieces to 180-grit, raising the grain between sanding with a damp cloth.

To assemble, I applied glue to the divider dadoes and to the tenons for the top. I slid the divider and the face panel into position before putting the top onto the tenons. Next I slid the bottom back panel into place, applied glue to the two bottom tenons, and put the bottom on the sides. While the glue was still fresh, I tapped the wedges into the tenon kerfs, being careful not to drive the wedges so far as to crack the top or bottom. I measured across the diagonals to make sure the carcase was square and then gave it a final sanding with 220-grit paper.

Frame-and-Panel Doors With Mitered Molding

The rails and stiles of the doors are molded with a quarter-round and fillet pattern along the inner edge. This molding, or sticking, is mitered, and the rails and stiles are joined with mortises and tenons. The top door is rabbeted to accept the glass and a glass stop, as shown in drawing detail A, and the bottom door is grooved for a flat, floating panel, as shown in drawing detail B on p. 57.

Aligning the mortises and tenons for the stiles and rails with the panel groove and the glass rabbet made it easier to cut the joints. The tenon is as thick as the panel groove is wide, so it is easy to cut a haunch on the tenon to fill the groove where it runs out the end of the stile, as shown in drawing detail B.

After assembling the doors, I glued and wedged in the turned knobs and mounted the doors to the carcase. When satisfied with the fit and alignment, I removed the hinges and finished the carcase and the doors, as described in the box on p. 59.

When the finish dried, I completed the clock by reinstalling the hinges, inserting the glass with glass stops, and mounting the face, works, and hands in the top. I used ³⁄₃₂-in.-thick, light restoration glass from S. A. Bendheim Co. (see "Sources") to give the clock an authentic antique appearance.

I had the face for my clock hand-painted on a sheet of tin by a local artist to duplicate the original. A variety of printed faces are also available from Klockit, Inc.

All that was left after sliding the upper back panel into its grooves and screwing it in place was to make a nice strip of Shaker pegs from which to hang the clock.

PHILIP C. LOWE designs, makes, and restores fine furniture in Beverly, Massachusetts.

Sources

Klockit
P.O. Box 636
N3211 County Road H
Lake Geneva, WI 53147
800-556-2548
www.klockit.com

S.A. Bendheim Co.
122 Hudson St.
New York, NY 10013
212-226-6370
www.originalrestorationglass.com

Johnson Paint
355 Newbury St.
Boston, MA 02115
800-404-8114
www.johnsonpaint.com
(for Sal-Soda)

Shaker Tall Clock

BY ROBERT TREANOR

Order, punctuality, and the timely completion of tasks were the rules of the day in Shaker communities. Even so, watches were considered inappropriate under the dictates of the faith. Tall clocks as well as wall-hung clocks were another story. They readily found a place in the community dwelling houses of the Shakers. Usually found in central hallways, tall clocks could be viewed easily by Shaker brothers and sisters as they went about their chores.

Shaker clocks, especially tall clocks, are most often associated with the Watervliet community in upstate New York. This is where Benjamin Youngs, a skilled clockmaker, became a convert to Shakerism. Youngs had been an apprentice to his father, a clockmaker in Hartford, Connecticut. Benjamin converted to the Shaker faith after he moved his family to a farm near the Watervliet community.

Brother Benjamin's early clocks, made before and shortly after his conversion, show an awareness of the fashion of the day. After his conversion, his clocks have the straightforward, functional, and modest properties associated with Shaker design.

THIS GRACEFUL CASE PIECE is made with readily available materials and simple techniques.

CASE JOINERY IS SIMPLE.
Sides are glued and nailed into rabbets cut in the case front. The back is screwed on, and the case is joined to the base with glue dowels.

You Don't Need Hard-to-Find Stock

The clock shown on p. 61 is based on one that's believed to be the work of Benjamin Youngs. That clock is illustrated in John Kassay's *The Book of Shaker Furniture* (University of Massachusetts Press, 1980). Kassay's measured drawings, in meticulous detail, give accurate dimensions of the parts down to 1/32 of an inch. I modified the dimensions slightly, so I could get the required parts from clear pine in nominal 1 in. thicknesses.

I can make this clock from standard lumberyard material, surfaced on all four sides (S4S), with only a small amount of waste. It pays to take your time at the lumberyard when selecting stock. Because some pieces, like the case front, are made with the full width of standard dimensioned material, you should pick only stock with straight, parallel sides. It's a good idea to take a straightedge with you to make sure the material is flat across its face.

The original clock was made with pine, and so is this one. The front and back of the case are made from 1x12s. The remaining parts are made from standard 1x10 and 1x8 pine. A painted finish is simple and authentic. I've also used hardwood with a clear finish.

Case Joinery Is Simple but Strong

I begin construction of the clock case by ripping the 6¼-in. sides from 1x10s, saving the rippings for later use. After carefully squaring the sides to length, I make a simple doweling jig (see the top photo on p. 64) from some square ¾-in. by ¾-in. material. The outside faces of the case sides must be exactly 11¼ in. apart. By orienting the jig along baselines accurately laid out on the case bottom and across the end grain of the case sides, I can bore holes guaranteed to align (see the center photo on p. 64). A stop on the drill bit prevents boring all the way through the bottom. I use ⅜-in. dowels, cutting them to length carefully so they don't bottom out in the holes.

The front of the case is made from the full width of a 1x12, which is actually 11¼ in. I attach the front to the sides with a nailed and glued rabbet joint. I often cut the rabbet at the tablesaw with a ¾-in.-wide dado head. But for this case, I used a router with a rabbeting bit. The rabbet is cut ¼ in. deep and runs the entire length of the front. Then I cut out the opening for the case door with a handheld scroll saw at the bench.

Simple Joinery for a Shaker Tall Clock

This Shaker clock case, based on an early 19th-century design, can be built with ¾-in.-thick dimensioned pine from the lumberyard. Just like the design, case and door joinery is uncomplicated.

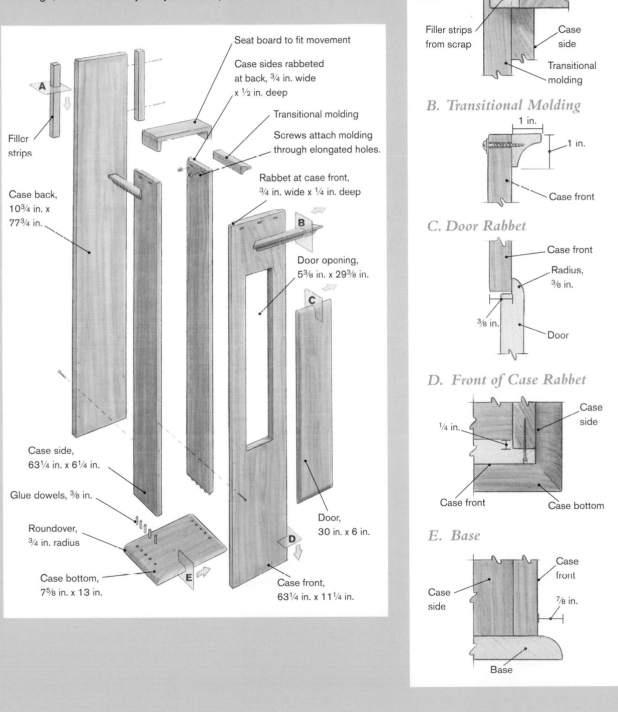

Seat board to fit movement

Case sides rabbeted at back, ¾ in. wide x ½ in. deep

Transitional molding

Screws attach molding through elongated holes.

Rabbet at case front, ¾ in. wide x ¼ in. deep

Filler strips

Case back, 10¾ in. x 77¾ in.

Door opening, 5⅜ in. x 29⅜ in.

Case side, 63¼ in. x 6¼ in.

Glue dowels, ⅜ in.

Roundover, ¾ in. radius

Case bottom, 7⅝ in. x 13 in.

Door, 30 in. x 6 in.

Case front, 63¼ in. x 11¼ in.

A. Filler Strips

Back

Filler strips from scrap

Case side

Transitional molding

B. Transitional Molding

1 in.

1 in.

Case front

C. Door Rabbet

Case front

Radius, ⅜ in.

⅜ in.

Door

D. Front of Case Rabbet

Case side

¼ in.

Case front

Case bottom

E. Base

Case front

Case side

⅞ in.

Base

DOWELING JIG. Holes bored in a hardwood scrap guide the bit as the author drills out a case side for glue dowels.

FLIP JIG AND DRILL BOTTOM. The jig, with its fence removed, is flipped over and aligned with layout lines on the case bottom to drill matching holes.

TEST-FIT. The jig ensures that dowels line up correctly, even if guide holes are not perfectly spaced or centered.

While the dado head is still in the saw, I cut rabbets in the back edge of the case sides to accommodate the back. I keep the width at ¾ in., but I increase the depth to ½ in. (I leave the back thickness at ¾ in., though it easily can be reduced to ½ in.) I rip the back to width from a 1x12. Ultimately, I will screw the back onto the case. Before doing so, I attach narrow filler strips, cut from the side rippings, to the top to span the gap created by the difference in width between the case and the hood.

Gluing Up the Case and Applying the Molding

Before gluing the case together, I round over the front and ends of the case bottom with a ¾-in.-radius router bit. I also give all case parts a preliminary sanding. You'll need a few long bar clamps to glue the dowel joints at the bottom of the case. The front is glued and nailed, and the back is simply screwed on. The front and back will help to hold the assembly square while the glue has time to dry. After the glue has dried and the nail holes have been filled, the case can be given its final sanding.

There was one part of this clock I couldn't cut from my standard material: the transitional cove molding attached to the top of the case. But in keeping with the frugal nature of this exercise, I took the molding from some rippings left over from a Windsor chair seat blank. I cut the molding profile with a ¾-in.-radius cove bit in the router. For safety's sake, I left the blank wide, cut the profile, and then ripped the molding to width.

Of the myriad ways to attach the molding, my choice was one of the simplest: gluing the miters and screwing the length of the molding to the case through slotted holes from the inside. Although there's no guarantee the miters will never open up, the slotted holes give the case a way

SLIDE-ON BONNET. The bonnet for this Shaker tall clock rests on transitional molding at the top of the case. It slides on and off to provide access to the clock's movement.

Building the Bonnet and Door

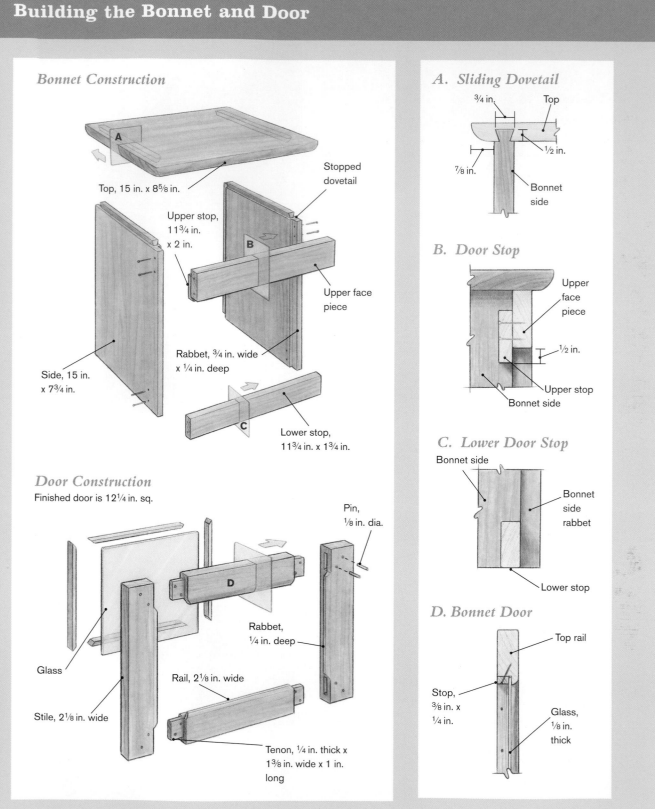

Bonnet Construction

Top, 15 in. x 8⅝ in.

A

Stopped dovetail

Upper stop, 11¾ in. x 2 in.

B

Upper face piece

Side, 15 in. x 7¾ in.

Rabbet, ¾ in. wide x ¼ in. deep

C

Lower stop, 11¾ in. x 1¾ in.

Door Construction

Finished door is 12¼ in. sq.

Pin, ⅛ in. dia.

D

Rabbet, ¼ in. deep

Glass

Rail, 2⅛ in. wide

Stile, 2⅛ in. wide

Tenon, ¼ in. thick x 1⅜ in. wide x 1 in. long

A. Sliding Dovetail

¾ in.

Top

½ in.

⅞ in.

Bonnet side

B. Door Stop

Upper face piece

½ in.

Upper stop

Bonnet side

C. Lower Door Stop

Bonnet side

Bonnet side rabbet

Lower stop

D. Bonnet Door

Top rail

Stop, ⅜ in. x ¼ in.

Glass, ⅛ in. thick

to expand and contract seasonally without cracking. The case door is lipped and rabbeted all the way around and attached with offset hinges, like those often found on kitchen cabinets.

Sliding Dovetails Join Hood Top and Sides

As with most tall clocks, the hood of this one is removable, providing access to the movement. After double-checking the dimensions, I cut the sides and top of the hood from a length of 1x10. The joint of the side to top easily could be the dowel joint used in the case, but for variety, I used a sliding dovetail on this clock (see the drawings on the facing page). Easily cut with a router inverted in a table, the sliding dovetail is a strong and appropriate joint.

Location of the joint is critical. The outside face of the hood sides must line up with the outside edge of the transitional molding. I mark the location of the joint on the underside of the hood top and set the height of the ¾-in. dovetail bit at ½ in. Then I carefully adjust the fence on the router table. With soft pine, there is no need to plow out a dado before cutting the dovetail; the joint is cut with one pass of the dovetail bit. A stop placed on the fence limits the length of the cut.

After cutting both ends of the top, I relocate the fence while the height of the bit remains constant. I extend the height of the fence to provide stability while cutting the hood sides. Using a piece of scrap pine the same thickness as the hood sides, I dicker with the fence until the joint is a firm press-fit. When satisfied, I cut the dovetails on the ends of the boards. Even though the dovetails extend across the entire width of the boards, the first inch closest to the front edge must be trimmed off for the rabbet cut into the inside faces of the sides.

FOR CLEAN MITERS, USE A GUIDE. Rabbets on door stiles and rails meet in a miter at inside corners. For tight-fitting joints, the author pares pieces with the help of a guide block cut to a 45° angle.

CLAMP AND PARE. With the rabbet cut away at the end of the door stile, the author pares the miter with a sharp chisel. The mitering tom plate is clamped to the stile along the layout line.

THE FIT IS RIGHT. The mitered rabbet at each corner is a pleasing construction detail and a practical means of building a door frame that will accommodate a piece of glass.

Sources

Frei & Borel

P.O. Box 796

Oakland, CA 94604

510-832-0355

www.ofrei.com

Olde Century Colors

54020 Andrews Ave.

New Carlisle, IL 46552

800-222-3092

www.oldecenturycolors-.com

Protect the Clock Movement From Dust

The rabbets cut into the inside faces on the sides have a double purpose. First, they act as a door stop, and second, they keep out dust, the main adversary of clock movements. I cut the rabbets in the same manner as I cut the ones in the clock case. Before gluing up the hood, I rout the front and ends of the top with the same roundover bit I had used on the case bottom.

The hood has no bottom, so for rigidity, I added a rail at the bottom of the hood behind the bottom door rail. I simply glue and nail the rail in place (see the drawing on p. 66). The upper rail, located above the door, is cut to fit within the rabbets and also is glued and nailed in place. An inner rail is glued and nailed behind the upper rail to act as a dust stop. The three rails are taken from what's left after ripping the case sides.

Hood Door Is Rabbeted for a Glass Insert

The hood door is assembled with the ubiquitous mortise-and-tenon joint. Because this clock has only one door, and a small one at that, I cut the joints by hand. After cutting the door parts to size from the rippings left over from the case sides, I lay out the joint using a square and a marking gauge. I rout the edge with a ¼-in. round-over bit and cut the rabbet for the glass before cutting the joint.

The joint is easily cut by boring out the mortise with a brace and bit and then clearing out the waste with sharp chisels. I use a backsaw to cut the tenons on the ends of the rails, first making the cheek cuts and then supporting the rails in a bench hook to make the shoulder cuts.

Trimming the miters at the joints requires a mitering template to guide the chisel (see the top photo on p. 67). With the template cut to an accurate 45° and set at the layout line, it's a simple matter to cut a perfectly fitting miter (see the center and bottom photos on p. 67). I make the door slightly oversize and trim it to a close fit after glue-up. Once I'm satisfied with the fit, I hang the door in the hood with simple butt hinges.

I bought the weight-driven eight-day movement for this clock from Frei and Borel (see "Sources," at left). It sits on top of a seat board made from three pieces of the wood I had left over. Appearing as the letter C sitting on its side, the seat board is attached to the ends of the case sides with dowels and without glue. Holes are bored into the seat for the pendulum as well as the weight chains. Another option would have been to extend the case sides and place a horizontal board bridging the sides where the movement would have been. The clock face, painted onto wood, is screwed to the seat board. The time ring on this dial is 7 in. dia. Paper dials are available from mail-order houses.

According to Kassay, the original clock was painted red, so I followed suit. I used Covered Bridge red paint available from Olde Century Colors (see "Sources").

ROBERT TREANOR, a former teacher in the woodworking program at San Francisco State University, builds and writes about furniture in the Bay area.

18th-Century Six-Board Chest

BY MIKE DUNBAR

This copy of a ca. 1800 blanket chest—also known as a six-board chest—is an ideal project for honing your woodworking skills. While the chest can be made by machine, its various parts are made equally well (and about as fast) by hand. It was fun to spend a few afternoons making something by hand. It reinforced for me how delightful the shop can be when the only noise is the whisk of sharp tools. I rediscovered how pleasant woodworking is without hearing, eye, and lung protection. When a storm knocked out the power one afternoon, I was able to keep working. It was delightful—just me, the wood, the tools, and the sunlight.

At first glance, the chest appears to be little more than a nailed box. As you make the project, you'll begin to respect simple joinery that requires mostly rabbets and dadoes. You'll begin to realize how much today's woodworking has developed construction into a design element. The original chest from which this one was copied has been in continuous use for nearly 200 years and is still solid and very much intact. Its survival is not unique. The chest

WHITE PINE CHEST MADE THE OLD WAY. Using sharp hand tools, the author made a blanket chest in a few afternoons. The till–a box within the box–is used to hold small items.

TWO-HANDED HANDSAWING. To avoid breaking a fragile edge, and thus making it difficult to restart a cut, hold the fingertips of your free hand lightly against the thin waste piece. To saw a square edge, stand directly above the cut so that you see the thin top edge of the saw, rather than either side of the blade.

cabinetmaker been working in another region, he might have used yellow poplar. I used 5/4 clear white pine. The original box was made when a 1-in. board was a full inch thick. I felt the proportions of the original were important to the chest's overall appearance, which is why I chose 5/4 stock. The exception is the chest's bottom panel, which I made from ¾-in.-thick #2 pine.

Jointing Stock, Gluing Panels

The original chest was made of six wide boards, excluding the three smaller pieces that make up the till, a small lidded compartment within the chest. Today, 18-in.-wide 5/4 pine is rare, so I bought 5/4x10 boards that could be glued up into six wide panels. Crosscut the stock 1 in. longer than the finished lengths of the panels so that when you glue them together, you won't have to worry about aligning the ends.

Like all hand-tool operations, cutting with a handsaw is easier when the wood is securely clamped to a bench. For me, it's easiest to follow my pencil line if, with each pull stroke of the saw, I raise the saw's teeth out of the kerf, away from the line, and then push them back into the line with each push stroke. This technique helps prevent the saw from wandering. To make a cut that's square to the face of the board, rather than one that is undercut or overcut, try to stand right over the saw. This way, when you look down, all you'll see is the thin top edge, not the face of either side of the blade (see the photo above).

Determine and mark the good side of each board—the side you want to face out—and pair up the pieces into panels. Place the paired-up boards together and clamp them in a vise for jointing. Jointing the two boards at the same time ensures that any variation from square on the two edges is equalized and that the finished panel will be flat (see the photos and drawings on the facing page).

seems to violate an important woodworking principle, in that the grain of the ends and sides is arranged in opposite directions. One would expect this to cause the front or back boards to split. However, that did not happen to the original example or to the untold numbers of other chests like it. Unlike glue, the nailing allows enough movement to compensate.

The original chest is generally referred to as a blanket chest, underscoring its purpose—to store folded items made of cloth. However, this was also a utilitarian piece of furniture usually kept in a bedroom against the wall or at the end of a bed. An average house would have several such chests.

The original piece's everyday function dictated a couple of construction choices for the cabinetmaker. Time-consuming joinery, like dovetails, was replaced with equally strong rabbeted joints. The original was made in New England, where white pine is still sold everywhere. Had the

Perfect Panels

Two edges at once. Boards that will be edge-glued into panels are folded into a vise so that facing sides are clamped against opposite jaws. Any off square-ness in the planed edge will be neutralized when the boards are married into a panel.

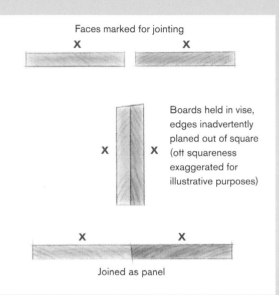

Faces marked for jointing

Boards held in vise, edges inadvertently planed out of square (ott squareness exaggerated for illustrative purposes)

Joined as panel

SPRING A JOINT. After jointing paired boards in a vise, take a final pass that begins and ends several inches from the boards' ends. When placed flat on a bench, the boards' edges will touch at each end and have a two-plane-shavings-wide gap in the middle (left). Two clamps will pull the gap together for glue-up (right).

Use a jointer plane to make the edges straight, which may take a little practice. The key is weight transfer; as you start a cut, exert more hand pressure on the plane's front knob. As you push the plane along the length of the board, transfer pressure to your other hand and to the rear of the plane. The long, straight sole of a jointer plane will remove only the boards' high spots. The first several passes you take will probably result in less-than-full-length curls of wood. Once you are able to plane a few full-length curls, sight along the boards for straightness or check them with a long straightedge.

Once the boards are straight, take a final pass with your plane, beginning about 3 in. from the front end of the boards and ending about 3 in. from the far end. This technique, called springing the joints, aids in gluing up boards. This incomplete pass creates a slight gap—two plane shavings wide—in the center of the boards when they are placed together on the bench for clamping. Because the boards touch at each end, one or two clamps spring the middle of the boards together.

Surface the Panels and Cut Them Square

Surface both sides of the panels to remove thickness-planer marks and to level the sides. As you plane, you'll find that what seemed like flat boards have lots of hollows. The panels are too long for a smooth plane. Its short sole will ride down into the hollows in the surface. I prefer a No. 6 jack plane, which is slightly longer and wider than a No. 5. For surface planing, use an iron with a slight crown honed into it. A crowned iron, as opposed to one with 90° corners between the cutting edge and the sides of the iron, reduces the likelihood of planing sharp ridges into the surfaces of the panels. Instead, the surface will be slightly scalloped, almost unnoticeably so, which is a sign of handplaned work.

One at a time, joint an edge of each panel. Use a framing square to lay out the ends prior to trimming. Lay out the finished width at the same time. Measure corner to corner to be sure the panel will be square; if the diagonal measurements are the same, the panel has four 90° corners. Cut the panels to size using a ripsaw along the length and a crosscut saw on the ends. When ripping, the saw's teeth should just touch the outside of the pencil line. This way, when you joint the edge to remove the saw marks, you will not be undersized.

Because the rough length of the boards are cut very close to the finished length of the glued-up panels, you'll be left with a thin strip to trim off each one. When using a handsaw, a slight twist of your wrist can break the thin strip, and trying to start the cut again in the middle of the edge can make it ragged and uneven. I like to use the fingertips of my free hand to push lightly against the strip to keep it from breaking (see the photo on p. 70).

Cut Boot-Jack Ends and the Stop Joint

The graceful, curved feet of the blanket chest are referred to as boot-jack ends because their shapes are similar to a once-common device used to help pull off boots by jamming the heel into the V.

To cut these ends, first make a template half the width of the chest's side and draw a curve that pleases your eye. After tracing the pattern ends of the chest, cut out the pattern using a small bowsaw (see the top photo on p. 74). The saw works best on the pull stroke. Use two hands and try to create a fluid motion that uses almost the entire length of the blade. Clean up the cuts using a spokeshave and a chisel, working from the center out on each side so as to cut with the grain.

Lay out the stop butt joint using a square and a marking gauge. Cut the return with a dovetail saw. Cut the length of the

Handmade Blanket Chest

Chests like this were as common as candles in period homes, which were notoriously devoid of closets. The chests were usually placed at the ends of beds and stored cloth goods. Local woods, available in wide boards, were used to make these chests. The boards were held together with rabbets, dadoes, and cut nails.

Blanket Chest Details

38³⁄₈ in. x 24 in. x 17 ³⁄₈ in.

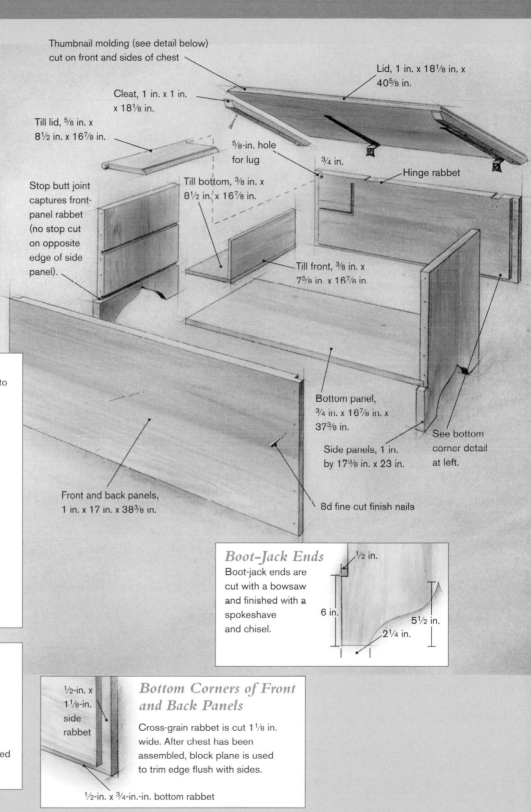

Thumbnail molding (see detail below) cut on front and sides of chest

Lid, 1 in. x 18¹⁄₈ in. x 40⁵⁄₈ in.

Cleat, 1 in. x 1 in. x 18¹⁄₈ in.

Till lid, ⁵⁄₈ in. x 8¹⁄₂ in. x 16⁷⁄₈ in.

⁵⁄₈-in. hole for lug

³⁄₄ in.

Hinge rabbet

Till bottom, ³⁄₈ in. x 8¹⁄₂ in. x 16⁷⁄₈ in.

Stop butt joint captures front-panel rabbet (no stop cut on opposite edge of side panel).

Till front, ³⁄₈ in. x 7⁵⁄₈ in. x 16⁷⁄₈ in.

Bottom panel, ³⁄₄ in. x 16⁷⁄₈ in. x 37³⁄₈ in.

Side panels, 1 in. by 17³⁄₈ in. x 23 in.

See bottom corner detail at left.

Front and back panels, 1 in. x 17 in. x 38³⁄₈ in.

8d fine cut finish nails

Till Construction

Back edge of lid is rounded over to conform to ⁹⁄₁₆-in. lug diameter.

⁵⁄₈ in.

³⁄₈ in.

Side panel

³⁄₈ in.

Lug, ⁹⁄₁₆ in.

³⁄₈ in.

³⁄₈ in.

³⁄₈-in.-deep groove

Till front butts bottom. Thumbnail on till lid is smaller than thumbnail on chest lid.

Thumbnail Molding on Chest Lid

¹⁄₈ in.

⁷⁄₈ in.

Rabbet plane is used to make ¹⁄₈-in.-deep cut, then edge is rounded over with block plane.

Boot-Jack Ends

Boot-jack ends are cut with a bowsaw and finished with a spokeshave and chisel.

¹⁄₂ in.

6 in.

5¹⁄₂ in.

2¹⁄₄ in.

Bottom Corners of Front and Back Panels

¹⁄₂-in. x 1¹⁄₈-in. side rabbet

Cross-grain rabbet is cut 1¹⁄₈ in. wide. After chest has been assembled, block plane is used to trim edge flush with sides.

¹⁄₂-in. x ³⁄₄-in.-in. bottom rabbet

BOWSAWED BOOT JACK. A plywood half pattern, seen on the uncut panel, is used to trace the boot-jack end that forms the blanket chest's feet. If the bowsaw jams in the cut, pop out the waste piece with a chisel blow to the panel's end grain.

SCRIBE WITH A KNIFE, then cut a dado with a chisel. Soft white pine, used for this chest and for thousands of similar antique versions, cuts easily with sharp hand tools. After a little chisel work, scribe again with the knife to cut cross-grain fibers until the dado is ½ in. deep.

joint with a fine ripsaw. The surface needs to be smoothed with a block plane to remove saw marks. By skewing a block plane, you can start close to the stop. Straighten out the plane as you continue the cut. Clean into the stop using a chisel. Test the joint with a straightedge.

Cut the Rabbets and Dadoes

The front and back of the blanket chest have a rabbet cut across the grain. An iron rabbet plane has an adjustable fence that regulates the width of the cut. Set the plane to cut a rabbet 1⅛ in. wide—wider than the 1-in. width of the sides. The face edge will overhang the sides slightly and can be planed smooth after the chest has been nailed together. The plane's depth stop regulates the depth of cut; set it to cut a ½-in.-deep rabbet. The plane has a scribe (also called a nicker) under the depth stop. The scribe looks like a rounded cross with one corner missing. Each corner is sharpened and, when placed into the opening, projects below the sole. It is used when cutting cross-grain. The scribe severs the wood fibers ahead of the cutter, eliminating dreaded tearout.

To avoid blowing out the end of a cross-grain rabbet, clamp a strip of sacrificial wood to the far side of the board you're cutting. And when starting a cross-grain rabbet, draw the plane backward so that the scribe makes a preliminary cut. When you push the plane, be sure to keep it square with the surface and end of the panel. You need to apply as much pressure in and down with the hand supporting the plane as you do with the one pushing it.

As the rabbet nears completion, the depth stop will begin to ride on the panel's surface. Usually, it comes in contact first on the side nearest you, as it is a natural tendency to decrease the pressure on the plane as your arms become extended. Make sure the rabbet has a consistent depth, then test the fit of the side panel into the rabbet. Cut all of the cross-grain rabbets, then cut the rabbets along the bottom of the front and back pieces to accommodate the chest's bottom panel.

The bottom panel of the chest also fits into dadoes cut in the side panels. In soft white pine, you can cut a dado very easily using a utility knife and a chisel (see the bottom photo on the facing page). Lay out the dado and clamp a straightedge along the mark. Score the line several times with a utility knife. Repeat on the other mark. With a chisel, pare the waste from the dado. When necessary, score the dado again and trim to depth.

Making the Till

Like most early blanket chests, this one has a till in one end. The till was used for storing small items that would be hard to find if placed in the chest itself. The till fits into stop dadoes cut in the front and back panels and in a dado on one side panel.

Surface-plane all till parts. Joint and cut them square. Thin wood presents a problem when cutting with a handsaw. The saws used in general work are too large and frequently break the piece. I own a number of small handsaws that are cut with 14 teeth per inch for small work.

The till has its own lid that hinges on two wood pins called lugs, which are made by removing all but a short rounded tenon from the lid's end-grain ends. Lay out the lugs with a try square and trace a ⁹⁄₁₆-in. circle on the end of each lug. Cut away the waste with a dovetail saw and a small handsaw. Clean up next to the lugs by paring away with a chisel. Using a chisel, undercut the waste on the corners of the square lugs (see the photo above). Pare away the waste to round the lug. Test its fit into a ⅝-in. hole drilled in a piece of scrap.

The till lid's front edge is molded with a very traditional profile known as a thumbnail. Make this molding the same way as those on the chest lid.

WOOD HINGE FOR THE TILL. After clamping the chest together for a test fit, mark the dadoes for the till. The till's lid hinges on lugs, small round tenons made by removing a strip of wood from each end of the lid and rounding off the remaining stub with a chisel.

Final Assembly Doesn't Require Glue

Use a square to lay out the dadoes for the till bottom and front, but do not cut them yet. First, test-assemble the chest. This not only allows you to check your joints but also to be sure that the stopped dadoes you've laid out will intersect. Run a clamp through the boot-jack ends to hold the bottom in place and the ends vertical. You can easily assemble the rest from this stage.

Disassemble and make any necessary adjustments. Cut the till dadoes the same way as those in the end pieces. Drill the ⅝-in. holes for the lugs in the locations shown.

Sources

Tremont Nail Co.
P.O. Box 111
Wareham, MA 02571
800-842-0560
www.tremontnail.com

Ball and Ball
463 W. Lincoln Hwy.
Exton, PA 19341
800-257-3711
www.ballandball-us.com

START THE THUMBNAIL WITH A RABBET PLANE; finish it with a block plane. The lid of the blanket chest has a thumbnail, a popular edge profile from the 18th century, on the two sides and the front. The thumbnail is made in two steps; first, cut a ⅜-in. rabbet, then round over the remaining square edge with a low-angle (12°) block plane.

When you're sure of the fit, reassemble the chest with the till parts in place and nail the rabbet joints. I used 8d fine-cut finish nails from Tremont Nail Co. (see "Sources," above). These nails look the same as those on the original chest.

Because the nails are visible, their spacing is important; use five nails per joint. Drill a ³⁄₁₆-in. pilot hole for each nail and run the long head with the grain.

Use a low-angle (12°) block plane to trim the rabbets' face edges flush with the chest ends. (Remember that you cut the rabbet joints wide on the front and back panels.)

Make and Fit the Lid

Cut the lid to size and make the cleats. Trace the beveled ends of the cleats with a bevel gauge set to the desired angle and cut them with a dovetail saw. Strike the bevels with a low-angle block plane to smooth away the saw marks.

To make the thumbnail molding, start with a rabbet plane to cut a ⅛-in.-deep rabbet on the lid's front and side edges. Again, it's a good idea to clamp a sacrifi-

cial waste block when planing end grain. Turn the rabbet into a thumbnail by using a block plane to round the square edge (see the photo above). Check to ensure that the profile is uniform along all edges. Attach the cleats using #10 by 1¼-in. screws.

The original chest had snipe hinges, which look like two cotter pins connected by their eyes. The leaves of the snipe hinges were drilled through the chest and clinched over into the wood. Some early blanket chests used butt hinges, while others used blacksmith-made offset strap hinges. Ball and Ball (see "Sources") sells the handsome wrought-iron reproduction strap hinges I used.

The location of the till makes it necessary to mount the hinges off center, a common practice in the 18th century. To mount the hinges, simply mark their locations on the chest, mortise the short leaves into the chest's back panel, and drive in a handful of black iron screws.

MIKE DUNBAR is a contributing editor to *Fine Woodworking* magazine.

A Shaker Blanket Chest

BY CHARLES DURFEE

DOVETAILS, FIGURED WOOD, and traditional moldings enhance this timeless piece.

The earliest storage chests were simple boxes made of six boards. As they evolved, a base, or plinth, was added to lift them off the floor and give them aesthetic appeal, while molding the edges created a more finished look. However, anyone who used such a chest soon found that they had to fish around for small items that ended up on the bottom. To solve this problem, furniture makers added first one drawer, and then two or even three drawers. Finally, the lid was eliminated, leaving a full chest of drawers as we know it today.

During the evolution from blanket box to chest of drawers, the grain in the sides changed from horizontal to vertical. Many of the single-drawer versions exhibit an

Dovetail the Chest

LAY OUT THE DOVETAILS. Use a pair of dividers to lay out the dovetails evenly. The spacing on the front corners may need to be slightly different from the spacing on the rear due to the presence of the drawer.

LINE UP THE BOARDS. Before laying out the pins, ensure that the boards are flat and meet at 90°.

EXTEND THE LAYOUT TO THE END OF THE BOARD. After marking the tails on the face of the board with a sliding bevel, extend the lines across the end of the board using a square and a knife. The knife cuts will help guide the saw as you cut.

MARK THE PINS FROM THE TAILS. With the boards secure, use a sharp pencil to transfer the location of the pins. A flashlight helps you see into the corners.

intermediate stage in this evolution, with vertical grain in the sides nailed to horizontal grain in the front, which probably is the only way they could be joined. In this piece, the older style with all horizontal grain is retained, which enables the front, back, and sides to be joined with dovetails. As long as the sides don't get too tall, this is a superior form of construction: Seasonal wood movement results in the parts moving together, instead of against each other.

Match the Dimensions to Your Hand-Picked Boards

Although the Shakers probably would have used painted pine, modern woodworkers may prefer the natural look of fine wood. I used some excellent single-log Pennsylvania cherry with lots of curl, nicely matched in grain and color.

You may need to adjust the overall dimensions if you want to use specific boards in particular places. In this case, I made the overall height a bit less than planned so that I could use an exceptionally fine single-width board for the front. You can lay out the actual dimensions on a story stick, using one face each for height, width, and depth. The story stick will give you all of the information necessary to begin construction, so you won't need any drawings.

After double-checking to ensure planning and layout make sense, mill and glue the boards for the front, sides, back, top, and drawer front. Leave the inner bottom oversize; it should be sized to just fit into its grooves. In addition, you can make up the bottom frame-and-panel. Remove any dry excess glue and flatten the boards using planes or sanders and a straightedge. To save time, I take the parts to a local mill shop and run them through a thickness sander.

With the case front, back, and sides cut to size, run the grooves for the inner bottom (on the front, the groove technically is a rabbet). The grooves need to be stopped before the ends and carefully aligned from the top so that all four grooves match up. I use a ¾-in. straight bit in a plunge router and run the tool against a straightedge to ensure a straight cut. Make the rabbet for the frame-and-panel bottom in the same fashion, stopped at the rear corners only.

Construct the Carcase with Dovetails

There are a lot of dovetails to cut in this project, so you might as well decide on a method of cutting them and stick with it. If you use a router setup, make sure the jig can handle the long row of the rear corners or has a way to index setups. I cut the dovetails with hand tools, which mostly is an exercise in sawing and marking accurately.

When laying out the joints, aim for a spacing between pins of about 1¾ in. on center. This chest has the peculiar problem of the front and back rows being different lengths, due to the drawer opening. Try to have the front series end with a small half pin or a small half tail, for appearance's sake. Make your scribe marks on the front edge of the sides down to the drawer opening only.

When cutting the dovetails, orient the outside face of the side toward you. Begin sawcuts at the top back corner; come across the top edge to set the saw in and then down the front face at an angle, keeping the saw completely in the kerf. Then finish the cut by raising the handle gradually. To ensure the cut is made to its full depth, I follow an old-timer's practice of cutting slightly past the scribe on the back side. After cutting the tails, check that they are square and do any necessary paring. In this way, any adjustments to get a good fit are done only on the pins.

Dovetailed Blanket Chest With a Drawer

Because of the drawer, the front corners have fewer dovetails than the rear corners. The dovetail spacing may be slightly different on the back than on the front but should appear to be the same.

Lipped-Front Drawer

The cherry drawer front is lipped on the top and sides. The sides, back, and bottom of the drawer are made of a secondary wood.

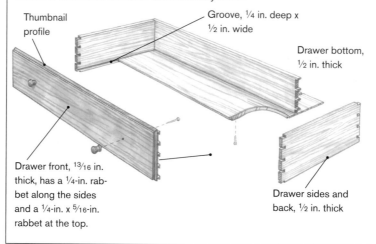

Thumbnail profile

Groove, ¼ in. deep x ½ in. wide

Drawer bottom, ½ in. thick

Drawer front, ¹³⁄₁₆ in. thick, has a ¼-in. rabbet along the sides and a ¼-in. x ⁵⁄₁₆-in. rabbet at the top.

Drawer sides and back, ½ in. thick

Front, ¾ in. thick x 13½ in. wide x 38 in. long

Rabbet, ¼ in. deep x ¾ in. wide

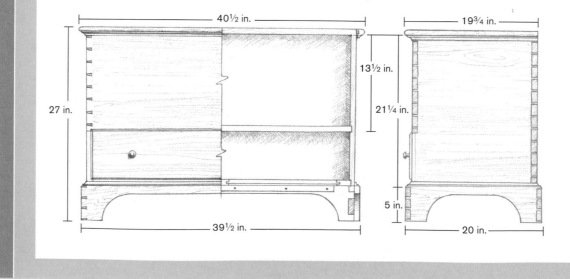

40½ in.

19¾ in.

13½ in.

21¼ in.

27 in.

5 in.

39½ in.

20 in.

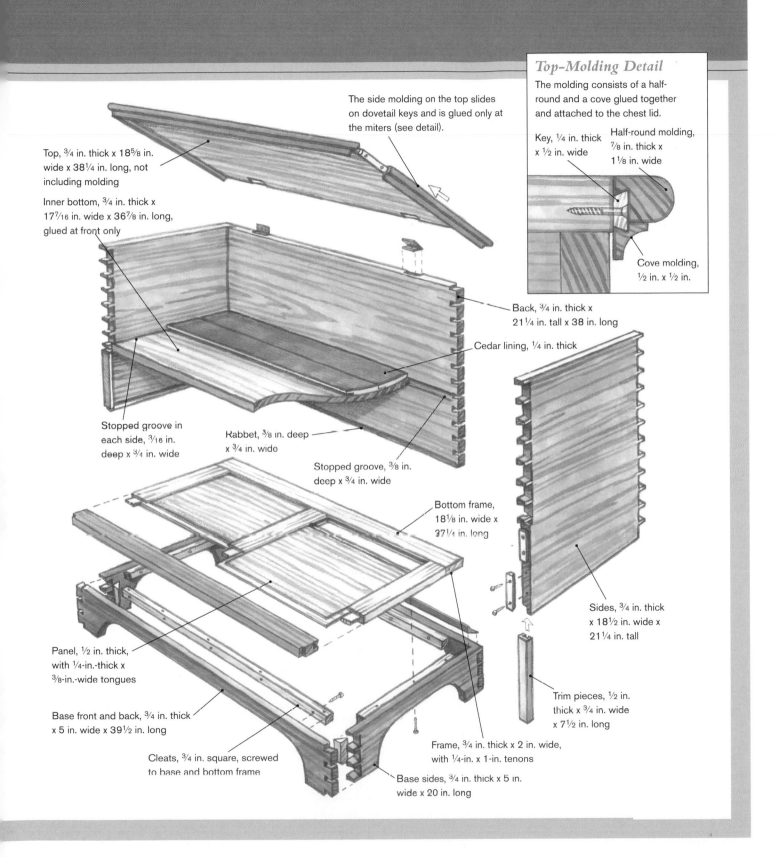

The side molding on the top slides on dovetail keys and is glued only at the miters (see detail).

Top, ³/₄ in. thick x 18⁵/₈ in. wide x 38¹/₄ in. long, not including molding

Inner bottom, ³/₄ in. thick x 17⁷/₁₆ in. wide x 36⁷/₈ in. long, glued at front only

Stopped groove in each side, ³/₁₆ in. deep x ³/₄ in. wide

Rabbet, ³/₈ in. deep x ³/₄ in. wide

Stopped groove, ³/₈ in. deep x ³/₄ in. wide

Panel, ¹/₂ in. thick, with ¹/₄-in.-thick x ³/₈-in.-wide tongues

Base front and back, ³/₄ in. thick x 5 in. wide x 39¹/₂ in. long

Cleats, ³/₄ in. square, screwed to base and bottom frame

Frame, ³/₄ in. thick x 2 in. wide, with ¹/₄-in. x 1-in. tenons

Base sides, ³/₄ in. thick x 5 in. wide x 20 in. long

Back, ³/₄ in. thick x 21¹/₄ in. tall x 38 in. long

Cedar lining, ¹/₄ in. thick

Bottom frame, 18¹/₈ in. wide x 37¹/₄ in. long

Sides, ³/₄ in. thick x 18¹/₂ in. wide x 21¹/₄ in. tall

Trim pieces, ¹/₂ in. thick x ³/₄ in. wide x 7¹/₂ in. long

Top-Molding Detail

The molding consists of a half-round and a cove glued together and attached to the chest lid.

Key, ¹/₄ in. thick x ¹/₂ in. wide

Half-round molding, ⁷/₈ in. thick x 1¹/₈ in. wide

Cove molding, ¹/₂ in. x ¹/₂ in.

When Things Go Wrong With Your Dovetails

Hand-cut dovetails should not be perfect, and indeed rarely will be. However, some faults that occur during fitting or assembly need to be repaired because they detract from the overall appearance of the piece.

WHEN A TEST FIT CRACKS THE WOOD. When dry-fitting dovetails, it takes only one pin that is too tight to cause a crack. This needs to be repaired before the two boards are dovetailed together. It's difficult to force glue down into the crack. But by placing the board half hanging off the bench and then flexing it while pushing the glue into the crack with your finger, you can work the glue in from both sides until the joint is saturated. Place waxed paper over the joint to protect the clamp that keeps the two sides of the crack parallel, and then place another clamp across the board to pull the crack together.

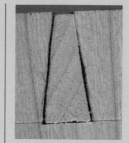

UNSIGHTLY GAPS BETWEEN PINS AND TAILS. Don't despair if there are gaps on either side of the pins and tails. If the gaps are very narrow, you can repair them by inserting some glue and peening the tail or pin with a ball-peen hammer. The blows spread out the end grain until it fills the gaps. This method requires that the tail or pin protrude at least ¹⁄₁₆ in., because it will be necessary to plane away the crushed surface end grain.

If the gaps are wide, the best way to fill them is by tapping in a thin wedge lubricated with a little glue. After the glue has dried, saw off the protruding part of the wedge and smooth the surface with a block plane. The end grain of the wedge will be an almost-perfect match with the pin or tail.

REPAIR A CRACK. While flexing the board up and down, force glue into the crack (right). Use one clamp to keep both sides of the crack aligned, with waxed paper between the glue and clamp; then close the crack with another clamp across the board (below).

PEEN SMALL GAPS. Small gaps can be filled by inserting a little glue and then hitting the pin or tail with a ball-peen hammer. Do this before planing the pins flush so that the hammer marks can be removed.

SHIM LARGER GAPS. A narrow wedge driven into the gap beside a pin will make an almost-invisible end-grain repair.

Assemble the Chest in Stages

Gluing this many dovetails is stressful enough without trying to do all of them at once. Before you start, make some cauls on the bandsaw to fit over the protruding pins. (1) First glue the front to the two sides and slide in the inner bottom, gluing the front edge into the rabbet and allowing the rest to float. (2) When this first assembly has dried, glue on the back, again using the cauls. (3) When the back is dry, fit and glue the frame-and-panel base into the bottom rabbet.

Use the Tails to Mark the Pins

When marking from one part to the next, make sure that the front and back are perfectly square to each side, and that the grooves line up so that the inner bottom will be able to slide in. I use a very sharp pencil lead extended from a lead holder for marking. It leaves a fine line, is much easier to see than a knife scribe, and doesn't accidentally cut the tail.

With the case dovetailing done, cut the recesses for the trim pieces on the lower front edges of the sides.

Dry-Fit the Carcase Before Final Assembly

When dry-fitting the case parts, push the joints together as much as possible by hand, then use a rubber mallet. When the joints are almost there, resort to clamps. You walk a fine line when fitting exposed dovetails: Too tight, and you risk splitting the wood; too loose, and you leave gaps between the pins and tails. Fortunately, splits and gaps can be fixed (as shown on the facing page).

For the glue-up, I make special clamp cauls (see the photos above) to span the pins because they protrude somewhat. To make the glue-up less nerve-racking, break down the process into steps. Assemble the front, the two sides, and the inner bottom

Cap the End Grain

To conceal the end grain, the sides are notched adjacent to the drawer, and trim pieces are attached over dovetail keys. (1) After assembling the case, notch the case bottom wthere it intersects the sides. (2) Then screw the dovetail key to the case using the trim piece to aid alignment. (3) Finally, saw apart the key to allow for seasonal movement of the case. Glue the trim piece only at the top.

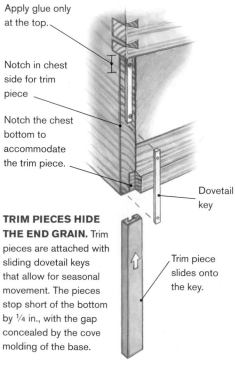

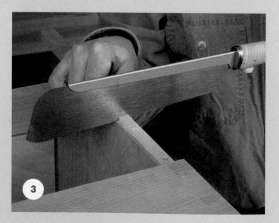

Apply glue only at the top.

Notch in chest side for trim piece

Notch the chest bottom to accommodate the trim piece.

Dovetail key

TRIM PIECES HIDE THE END GRAIN. Trim pieces are attached with sliding dovetail keys that allow for seasonal movement. The pieces stop short of the bottom by ¼ in., with the gap concealed by the cove molding of the base.

Trim piece slides onto the key.

as a unit first. The front edge of the inner bottom is glued only to the front rabbet (the rest is unglued to allow for seasonal movement). If necessary, cut a temporary spacer to hold the rear edges in the correct alignment. The second step is to glue on the back. When the back is dry, fit and glue the base frame into the bottom rabbet.

Conceal the End Grain With Trim Pieces

With the carcase assembled, cut a notch in the base frame at each front corner for the trim pieces. On original Shaker chests, these trim pieces as well as the moldings simply were nailed on, which not only caused seasonal wood-movement problems but also were aesthetically unpleasing in an unpainted piece. A more elegant solution is to attach these cross-grain parts with sliding dovetail keys. I vary this method slightly, screwing the key on beginning at the inboard end and pulling off the molding, fastening as I go. The segments are cut out and the molding slid back on with glue at the inboard end. Leave the bottom end of the trim pieces about ¼ in. short of the case bottom to allow for seasonal expansion. The cove molding will cover the gap.

Build the Base and the Top Before Attaching the Molding

On this chest, the base runs around all four sides, as opposed to most early-American chests that have bracket bases on the front and sides only. Saw the dovetails first, and then cut out the profile on the bandsaw; you can save the cutouts to use as clamp cauls. Nail a plywood template to the back of the base pieces and clean up the profile on the router table with a top-guided bearing bit. Screw cleats to the inside of the base and drive screws through the cleats to attach the base to the chest.

Because the moldings overlap the top edge of the case, the top should be sized so that the front clearance is proportional to the amount of seasonal wood movement. I built this chest in the winter, and the wood's moisture content was 6%, so I sized the top with a minimal clearance of a strong 1/16 in. (3/16 in. to 1/4 in. should be sufficient clearance for a summer-built chest).

The top molding consists of a half-round and a cove made on the router table and then glued together. While you're at it, make some extra cove molding for the base. The front piece is mitered and glued to the top, while the sides are installed over dovetail keys, with glue at the miters only.

The drawer front is in the traditional style, lipped on the top and sides and molded all around. The sides and back on my drawer are quartersawn pine, and the bottom is poplar. You can find quartered stock at any lumberyard—just look through a stack of boards for ones with growth rings perpendicular to the board's face.

Cut the drawer front first, with its side rabbets trimmed so that they just fit into the opening. The top rabbet needs to have only about 1/16 in. of clearance, because seasonal movement of the drawer will be in the same direction as the case. Cut the dovetails by hand, but use a Forstner bit to drill out the bulk of the waste between the half-blind pins.

Attach the Hardware and Finish the Piece

By now you will have something that looks like a chest. The top is secured with mortised-in butt hinges. I used extruded-brass hinges from Whitechapel (see "Sources" on p. 86), but you may opt for a more authentic style with thinner leaves. When the top is fastened, find the location for the stay. I used a brass chain, which isn't strictly traditional Shaker but still shares a similar simplicity.

Throughout the construction process, you should have been planing, scraping,

Sources

Whitechapel
P.O. Box 11719
Jackson, WY 83002
307-739-9478
www.whitechapel-ltd.com

and/or sanding to all but the final passes. I generally take out machine marks (including the tracks left by the thickness sander) with a handplane and scraper. The final work is done with a 220-grit disk in a random-orbit sander.

I used Minwax® Antique Oil Finish, but any oil/varnish mixture will work well. The first coat is always exciting—the figure fairly jumps off the surface—but it also reveals any dents, dings, and glue splotches that should be wet-sanded with finish using 220- or higher-grit sandpaper.

After the finishing is completed, add the thin cedar lining in the chest bottom. I used some leftover western red cedar clapboards. I planed them down, shiplapped the edges, and tacked them in, leaving them unfinished. Years hence, a light sanding will refresh the smell, allowing me to recall the pleasure of building this piece.

CHARLES DURFEE builds furniture in Woolwich, Maine.

Install the Bracket Base

SAVE THE WASTE PIECE. After cutting the profile of the base, save the offcuts, which can be cut in two and used as clamtping cauls when gluing together the base.

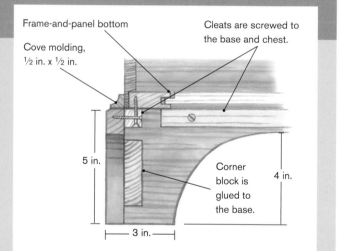

Frame-and-panel bottom

Cove molding, ½ in. x ½ in.

Cleats are screwed to the base and chest.

Corner block is glued to the base.

5 in.

4 in.

3 in.

ATTACH THE CLEATS. Screw cleats to all four sides of the base. Then drive screws up through each cleat to attach the base to the chest.

FIT THE MOLDING. Because the grain on the chest runs horizontally, the base molding can be glued to both the base and the sides.

Captain's Desk Is Compact and Efficient

BY CAMERON RUSSELL

Originally designed for cramped ship's quarters, captain's desks pack a lot into a small space. In addition to the writing surface and drawer storage, this desk has a compartment for large items behind a hinged door and a lockable compartment beneath the inlaid leather writing surface.

I decided to build my desk in a series of individual components: the desk box and writing surface, the frame-and-panel drawer case, the door and drawers, the columns, the base frame, and the feet. The components can be made in any order, finished, and then assembled into the completed desk.

The desk is also one of my favorite pieces because its components require a variety of joinery techniques and furniture-making skills: dovetail joints for drawers and the desk box, mortises and tenons for the frame members, lathe turning between centers and with a faceplate, hinge setting, insetting leather (see the sidebar on pp. 90–91) and installing a lock and escutcheon.

A CAPTAIN'S DESK IS HIGHLY FUNCTIONAL, providing a variety of storage in a compact piece. Also called a davenport, after the sea captain who commissioned a similar piece in the late 18th century, this desk presents a variety of joinery challenges, from mortises and tenons to half-blind mitered dovetails.

A Captain's Desk

This project provides plenty of storage in a small space and also provides opportunity for lots of joinery practice.

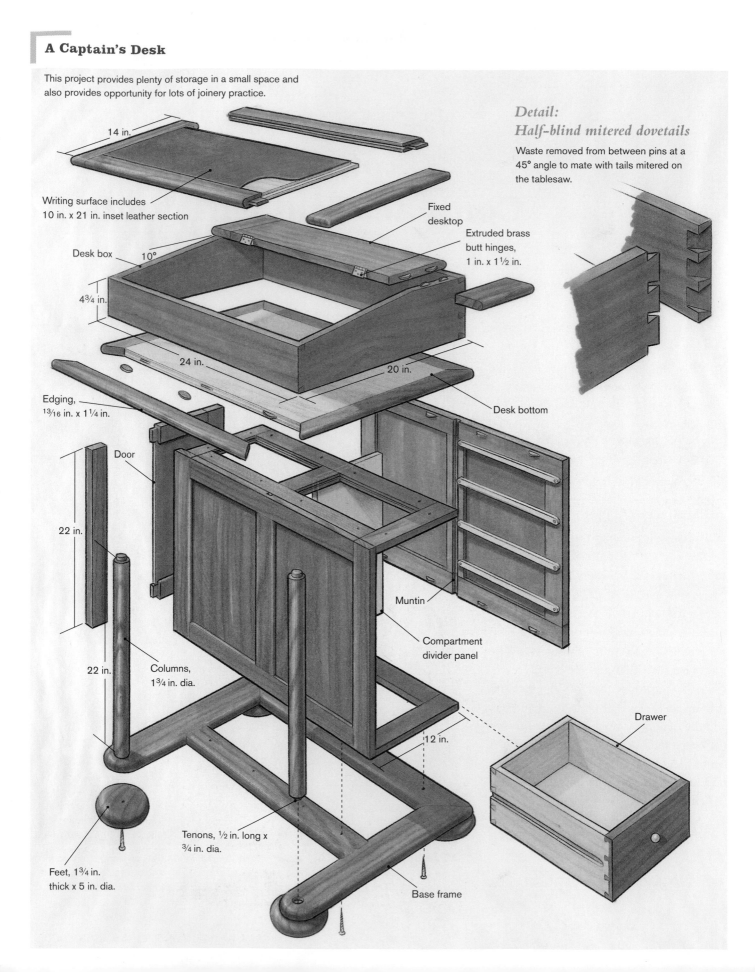

14 in.

Detail:
Half-blind mitered dovetails

Waste removed from between pins at a 45° angle to mate with tails mitered on the tablesaw.

Writing surface includes 10 in. x 21 in. inset leather section

Desk box

10°

4¾ in.

Fixed desktop

Extruded brass butt hinges, 1 in. x 1½ in.

24 in.

20 in.

Edging, 1³⁄₁₆ in. x 1¼ in.

Desk bottom

Door

22 in.

Muntin

Compartment divider panel

22 in.

Columns, 1¾ in. dia.

12 in.

Drawer

Feet, 1¾ in. thick x 5 in. dia.

Tenons, ½ in. long x ¾ in. dia.

Base frame

The Desk Box

The lockable desk box is joined with half-blind mitered dovetails and has a hinged lid that rests on angled sides to form a comfortable writing surface. To get the slant of the right and left sides identical, I joined them with double-faced tape. I then marked out the 10° slope on the sides, bandsawed, and planed them smooth.

I used half-blind mitered dovetails to join the desk box because this joint is strong, provides the exposed joinery that goes with the vague nautical theme, and lets the grain pattern wrap around the box. To cut this joint, I mark and saw the tails first with the ends of the sides still square as in a normal dovetail joint. I then use the tails as templates to mark out the pins on the ends of the front and back pieces.

After the tails have served as templates, I miter the sides on a tablesaw crosscut tray. I cut the pins in the front and back of the box by sawing to a 45° angle from the line that will become the inside corner out to the outside corner. The waste between pins is chiseled and pared carefully to mate with the mitered tail ends (see the detail on the facing page).

The desk bottom is a plywood panel framed by $^{13}/_{16}$-in.-thick edge strips mitered at the corners. The edge strips are shaped from both faces with a $^3/_8$-in.-radius round-over bit mounted in a router table.

The fixed desktop is made breadboard-style with end caps biscuit-joined to the top. Because the top is only 7 in. wide and mahogany is a relatively stable wood, this cross-grain construction hasn't been a problem. The front edge of the fixed top is beveled 5° to match a corresponding bevel on the upper edge of the writing surface. Combined, these bevels allow the slanted writing surface to rest flat on the 10° tapered sides of the desk box with no gap at the hinge joint.

The desk-box top and bottom are secured to the box with biscuits and screws, as shown in the drawing on the facing page. Before gluing the box, I applied masking tape to the insides of corners. When the inevitable glue beads oozed out, they formed on the taped surface, not the wood. I stripped the tape off while the glue was still tacky and managed to avoid any further cleanup.

The Writing Surface

The writing surface is composed of a leather-covered panel secured in a mortised-and-tenoned stile and rail frame. A ¼-in.-wide groove runs around the inside edge of the frame to house the rabbeted edge of a ½-in.-thick plywood panel. Because leather thickness varies, have the leather on hand, so you can position the panel groove to keep the leather flush with the surrounding frame. I veneered the bottom face of the plywood panel with Honduras mahogany to match the rest of the desk. After the writing surface frame and panel has

VERTICAL STORAGE. Originally used to store sea charts, the large compartment behind the hinged door is great for wall maps, posters, or other items that won't fit in the drawers on the opposite side of the desk.

Leather is a great material for a writing surface. Its texture provides the right combination of support and cushioning to give handwriting a pleasurable feel. And because this desk is so small, the required leather should be available from most craft-supply stores or from Berman Leathercraft, Inc. (25 Melcher St., Boston, Mass. 02210; 617-426-0870).

Selecting and preparing leather–For a writing surface, top-grain leather (the most expensive kind) is not necessary. The most critical factor is choosing a color to complement the wood tones.

Trim the leather with a sharp knife, leaving about ½ in. extra material on each side. Moisten the face side of the leather by lightly spraying it with water from the kind of squeeze bottle used to mist houseplants. Flip the leather over onto a clean piece of unprinted paper, and it's ready for gluing.

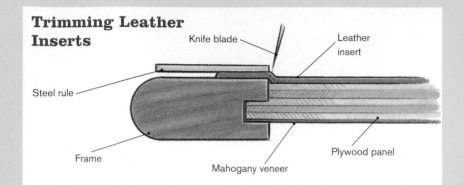

Trimming Leather Inserts

Knife blade — Leather insert — Steel rule — Frame — Mahogany veneer — Plywood panel

Preparing the leather paste–To glue up the leather, I use a special paste made from laundry starch, alum, powdered chalk, wintergreen, and water. White or yellow glues don't allow enough time to position the leather, and they also can make the leather hard or stain it by seeping through the leather's pores. I have also tried plastic resin glues, and I have had the same problems with them.

Laundry starch (4 tablespoons), the kind used to starch table linens, is the main ingredient of my special leather paste. If you can't find starch in a large supermarket, try a commercial laundry that caters to restaurants. Powdered alum (½ teaspoon), which I've found in the spice rack of the supermarket, is a salt that helps the paste grip the leather. Powdered white chalk (1 tablespoon), such as that used in a carpenter's chalkline, is added as a thickener. Finally, oil of wintergreen (three or four drops), available from most pharmacies, helps discourage the growth of fungal bacteria. Although the wintergreen is not a vital ingredient, it makes the shop smell like a candy store, and it helps prevent break-

received its final finish coat, the leather is inlaid into the recessed panel (see the sidebar above).

Installing the Hardware

The writing surface is hinged to the fixed desktop with brass butt hinges that are let equally into each piece. A chest lock mortised inside the box secures the writing surface to the box. I roughed out the lock mortise with a small straight bit in a laminate-trimming router and then cleaned up the edges with a chisel.

Mass Production Techniques for the Drawer Case Parts

The main box that forms the body of the desk houses drawers in one side and a door-covered storage compartment in the other. The front and back of the box are identical frame-and-panel assemblies, each consisting of two stiles stretching the entire vertical height, two rails, a muntin (a single center divider), and two panels. The door is also a frame-and-panel assembly built of the same dimensioned stock as the front down of the leather, especially in moist environments.

Mix the ingredients listed above in a wide-mouth glass jar. Slowly add boiling water until the mixture is about the consistency of paint.

Pour the water as slowly as possible and stir vigorously to avoid lumps. Once the ingredients are mixed to a creamy consistency, stop adding water, and heat the jar in a pan of water over a low heat.

Continue stirring. Before long, the starch should react, and the mixture will suddenly turn into a paste.

Place a lid on the jar, and the paste will remain usable for several hours.

Gluing on the leather–Spread the paste evenly on the underside of the moistened leather, working from the middle out to the edges to ensure an even stretch to the pliable moist leather. Once fully pasted, fold the pasted side over on itself to prevent drying out while you work on the wood surface.

Brush a layer of paste on the wood at about the same rate as if you were painting it. Unfold the leather on the wood backing, and press it in place using your fingertips, working from the center out to the edges. The slow-setting paste allows the leather to slide and shift as required. Once the leather has been worked out to the sides of the recess, use your thumbnail to crease a line in the leather where the frame meets the backing board.

The next step is probably the most critical in getting a neat job. Hold a straightedge on the waste side of the leather directly above the crease line. Draw a sharp knife along the straightedge angled in about 5° or 10°, as shown in the drawing on the facing page. If done correctly, the leather edge should neatly tuck up to the frame. Once trimmed and tucked, wipe any excess paste from the frame and leather with a damp cloth. Allow the panel to sit overnight to give the paste a chance to dry before applying the dressing.

Dressing the leather–I rub in a special home-brewed dressing to give the leather a rich sheen. To blend my dressing, I mix two parts anhydrous lanolin (an ingredient found in many skin-care and cosmetic products and usually available at well-stocked pharmacies) and three parts neatsfoot oil, a traditional leather preserving oil. I rub the dressing vigorously into the leather with my fingertips. The friction from my hands melts the lanolin and works it deep into the pores of the leather. When the leather is saturated, I wipe off the excess and buff the surface with a soft flannel cloth. The dressing can be applied every year or whenever the leather appears to lose its luster. Avoid too much dressing, though, or a greasy film may begin to build.

and back panels. The top and bottom of the drawer case are web frame assemblies identical to one another except for one detail. The door-covered compartment has a plywood floor let into grooves in the frame.

All of the frame pieces are ¾ in. thick by 1¾ in. wide, so I milled all this stock and cut the joinery at one time. I used ¼-in. by ¼-in. grooves for all the panels and 1-in.-deep mortises for all the joints. When the milling operations were complete, I dry-assembled the frames to test the joinery. While the frames were assembled, I marked each joint, so I could round over the edges without cutting into the joint area. I then milled each piece separately on the router table, being careful to stop shy of my marks. I assembled the frames (including the panels, which can be solid wood or veneered plywood or composition board) and used a chisel and a fine file to extend the round-overs into a crisp corner. This detail took surprisingly little time and added another hand-crafted touch to the desk.

I attached the drawer guides before the drawer case was assembled because there was more room to work. I made up blocks to locate the guides while I screwed them in place.

All the rails, stiles, and muntins of the top and bottom web frames have grooves cut around the inside edges. The grooves house a rabbeted ½-in.-thick plywood floor panel for the storage compartment and mate with ¼-in.-long stub tenons on the ends of the rails and muntins that hold the frames together. With the web frames assembled, I routed grooves along the muntins and across each rail to house the compartment divider.

I cut biscuit joints to attach the top and bottom web frames to the front and back panels and then dry-assembled the pieces. When everything fit properly, I dis-assembled, sanded, and finished all the components. The only drawback to applying a finish at this stage is that glue surfaces must be protected by masking. This small effort is a good trade-off for the ease of working on flat surfaces versus applying finish inside a small box. And, as an added bonus, the quality of finish will be much better.

Making the Drawers

The drawers are traditionally joined with through-dovetails at the back and half-blind dovetails at the front. The ¼-in.-thick ply-wood bottoms slide under the back and into grooves in the side and front. I made up pads of upholstery fabric covering ½-in.-thick foam and ⅛-in.-thick plywood to cover the drawer bottoms and the writing compartment floor as well. This feature not only looks rich but also allows small items to be picked up more easily.

Turning Columns and Feet and Adding a Base Frame

I turned two cylindrical columns to connect the desk box and the base frame, as shown in the drawing on p. 88. The shoulder-to-shoulder length of the columns is the same as the height of the drawer case.

The base frame is a large U-shaped structure mitered in each corner with an additional cross member under the front side of the drawer case. I used biscuits to join all of the frame pieces, but before assembly, I bandsawed and sanded the open ends of the frame to their half-round shape.

The four round feet are blocks that I bandsawed to rough shape and then turned and sanded on a lathe. I used a plywood template to check my turning progress. Again, I countersunk screws through the bottom of the feet and fastened them to the base frame. When the desk was entirely assembled, I then covered the screw heads with felt pads on the feet bottoms.

Finished With a Special Mix

The finish used on this desk was an oil mixture made of equal parts tung oil, boiled linseed oil, and gloss urethane. I find this mixture penetrates like any oil finish but builds up quickly because of the urethane. I allowed the first coat to penetrate the wood for 20 minutes, reapplying in any areas that soaked in and became dry. After 20 minutes, I wiped off all of the excess oil and disposed of the rag in a fireproof container. The following day, I rubbed in the oil-urethane mixture using 400-grit silicon car-bide wet-or-dry sandpaper. Again, I wiped off the excess oil and let it dry overnight. The 400-grit application was repeated for another two or three days followed by a few days of 600-grit applications. Finally, when the oiling was completed and the entire desk assembled, the whole piece was waxed with a mahogany-colored paste wax. This final step really highlighted all of the half-round moldings from the top right down to the feet.

CAMERON RUSSELL is a furniture-making and design instructor at Camosun College in Victoria, British Columbia, Canada.

Cherry Chest of Drawers

My daughter Anna, going on 3 years old, loves to dress up. But picking out her own clothes means she has to deal with the cumbersome drawers of the flea-market dresser in her room.

After she had an especially frustrating day wrestling with those drawers, I decided she needed a new place for her clothes. So I made her a simple dresser with seven drawers in four rows, with each row graduated in size and each drawer outlined with

BY MICHAEL PEKOVICH

DOVETAIL JOINERY DECORATES this Shaker-inspired case piece.

Dovetail Shortcuts on the Tablesaw

The carcase top and bottom require dovetails of different lengths. To save time and reduce the number of setups, Pekovich cuts dovetails of equal lengths on both pieces, then trims the bottom dovetails later.

THE TABLESAW SAVES TIME. The tails on the top and bottom panels are cut using a tablesaw blade with the teeth ground to the angle of the dovetail.

RABBET HELPS ALIGN THE DOVETAILS DURING MARKING AND ASSEMBLY. The 1/8-in.-deep rabbet extends to the baseline of the tails.

FINALLY, TRIM 1/8 IN. FROM EACH END OF THE CASE BOTTOM. Shorter tails are necessary for the half-blind dovetail joint at the bottom of the case.

The Carcase Begins as a Dovetailed Box

The top is joined to the sides with through-dovetails, which will be partially concealed by molding. The bottom is attached with half-blind dovetails.

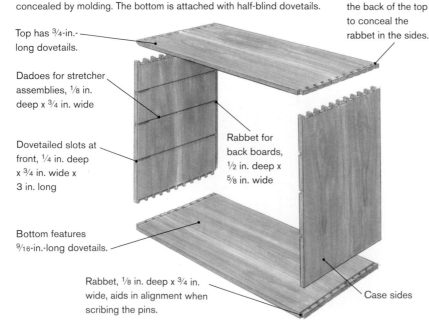

Top has 3/4-in.-long dovetails.

Dadoes for stretcher assemblies, 1/8 in. deep x 3/4 in. wide

Dovetailed slots at front, 1/4 in. deep x 3/4 in. wide x 3 in. long

Bottom features 9/16-in.-long dovetails.

Rabbet, 1/8 in. deep x 3/4 in. wide, aids in alignment when scribing the pins.

Leave a half tail at the back of the top to conceal the rabbet in the sides.

Rabbet for back boards, 1/2 in. deep x 5/8 in. wide

Case sides

a thumbnail profile. The bracket base is decorated with dovetails at the corners, which echo the exposed dovetails at the top of the case. These small details, along with some carefully chosen lumber, complete the ornamentation.

There's a lot to consider when designing a chest of drawers, and the look you choose will affect your construction method. In this case, my decision to expose the dovetails at the top of the case required a molding applied around the edges of the top, which in turn required an extra drawer stretcher attached behind that top molding. When it comes to design decisions, this domino effect is common, and it's a big reason why I try to figure out the details on paper before I begin to build.

Top-Quality Lumber Is Square One

Like many woodworkers, I've made the mistake of trying to save money by choosing lesser-quality lumber, working around knots and sapwood, and gluing up lots of narrow boards. I've come to realize that the investment in materials is small compared to the investment in labor.

For this piece, I purchased lumber from Irion Lumber Co. (see "Sources" on p. 104), a mail-order dealer in Pennsylvania. The supplier found multiple boards from the same tree, saving me the trouble of dyeing or staining mismatched boards. The total cost of the roughly 125 bd. ft. of lumber, including shipping, was $685★, about $20 more than what my local lumberyard would have charged.

Dimension Lumber as You Go

Things go wrong when I follow strict measurements. For this project, I started with the overall dimensions in the cut list and adjusted some of the measurements as I worked. To this end, you must be careful not to dimension all of the parts ahead of time, because some parts, such as the drawer stretchers, may change in dimension slightly as you go. When sizing the case, the important thing is that corresponding parts match. The pieces also must be cut square and glued up square. The foundation of the dresser is its carcase; as it goes, so goes the rest of the project.

Flat panels are a must The carcase of the dresser may be just a dovetailed box, but it's big and cumbersome. The various parts must be glued up into panels and surfaced before you can work on the joinery. Begin with 4/4 rough stock and shoot for a finished thickness of between ¾ in. and ⅞ in. Glue up the boards into larger panels, and take the time to get the panels as flat as possible. It will save time later.

Cut Pins on the Case Sides

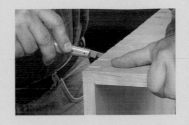

MARK THE PINS WITH A KNIFE. The rabbet helps align the large panels for marking. Cut along the scribe lines with a backsaw.

COPE AND ROUT OUT THE WASTE BETWEEN THE PINS. Clamp a support block to the workpiece and rout close to the sawkerf with a ¼-in. straight bit. Chisel away any remaining waste.

ADD A FENCE TO THE ROUTER FOR HALF-BLIND PINS. The bit depth establishes the dovetail depth while the fence sets the height (left). A pair of skew chisels help clean out the corners (right).

Use a Jig to Rout Dadoes and Dovetailed Slots

ROUTER JIG ALIGNS CARCASE DADOES. The simple jig made from ³⁄₄-in.-thick poplar is sized to fit your router's base. Align the jig with layout marks on the case side and clamp it securely. Use a ³⁄₄-in. straight bit to rout the ¹⁄₈-in.-deep dadoes for the drawer runners.

THE SAME JIG IS USED FOR DOVETAILED SLOTS. After routing all of the dadoes, use a ³⁄₄-in. dovetail bit to cut slots for the front and back drawer stretchers.

When it comes to surfacing the case parts, I don't mind getting out a handplane and scraper and working up a sweat. But you might want to think about locating a cabinet shop or lumberyard in your area that will rent time on a wide belt sander. These big machines can flatten panels in a hurry; the cost for sanding these four panels would have been around $40.

Once the case sides, top, and bottom have been surfaced, it's time to start building the carcase.

Assemble the Carcase With Dovetails

I normally cut dovetails by hand, but the large number required for this project prompted me to look to machines for help in speeding the process.

I cut the tails in the carcase (as well as in the drawer sides) using a tablesaw blade ground especially for the purpose. Then I removed most of the waste with a coping saw and pared to the baseline with a chisel. I scribed the pins with a knife and cut them with a backsaw, but I used a router to remove most of the waste. The final result has the look of handsawn dovetails but without the drudgery.

In this dresser, the case top is joined to the sides with through-dovetails, while the bottom is joined with half-blind dovetails. This design requires that the top and bottom have dovetails of different lengths, which means that the bottom will be shorter than the top but must be precisely the same length between the bases of the dovetails. To ensure that everything ends up square, you need to crosscut the case top and bottom to the same size and cut tails of equal length on each piece. The bottom tails will be trimmed later.

To accommodate the shiplapped back, the sides are rabbeted. So you must exercise care when laying out the dovetails along the top to avoid exposing the rabbets in the case sides.

After cutting the tails, run a shallow rabbet (about ⅛ in. deep) the length of the tails along each end of the case top and bottom. This shallow rabbet helps keep the case parts in alignment while you scribe the pins on the case sides. Now trim ⅛ in. off each end of the bottom piece. This method ensures that the distance between the base of the dovetails on the top and the bottom is equal.

To lay out the pins, clamp the case side to be scribed in the front vise of a bench, and clamp the other case side along the rear apron of the bench; this serves to support the top and bottom panels while marking. Snug up the rabbet on the case top (or bottom) to the case side and use a marking knife to scribe the pins. Then saw right along the line. Remove the waste between the pins using a router equipped with a ¼-in. straight bit, and clean up with a chisel.

Rout Dadoes for Drawer Partitions Before Gluing Up the Case

Prior to gluing up the case, you need to rout the dadoes and the stopped-dovetail slots for the stretchers, runners, and dividers.

Install Drawer Frames After Glue-Up

ROUT DOVETAILS ON THE FRONT AND BACK STRETCHERS. Use the same bit that was used for the slots in the case. A horizontally mounted router allows the workpiece to remain flat on the router table.

INSTALLING THE DRAWER FRAMES. Begin by gluing the front stretchers in place (left). Then flip over the case and insert the runners into the front stretchers, applying glue only at the front tenons (right). Finally, glue the back stretchers into place.

Mount the Carcase on a Bracket Base

THE CORNER JOINTS COMBINE DOVETAILS WITH A MITER AT THE TOP (above). The miter allows for the rabbet on the inside edge that supports the case, as well as the decorative chamfer along the outside edge. To mount the base, glue on blocks that can be screwed to the carcase (right). Elongate the middle and rear screw holes to allow for seasonal movement.

Rout all of the dadoes the full width of the sides using a ¾-in. straight bit. A simple jig can help guide your router. The base of my router is not perfectly concentric to the collet, so I marked an X on the base, making sure the X sat on the right side of the jig while routing. This ensured that the dovetail keys would align with the dadoes. Rout 3-in.-long stopped dovetails at the ends of each dado using a ¾-in. dovetail bit.

To prevent clamps from marring the case during glue-up, make a set of cauls for each corner. Notch the cauls to fit around the dovetail pins and secure them to the case using double-faced tape to prevent shifting. After the case is clamped, check for square with a tape measure.

Stretcher Systems Support the Drawers

Once the case has been glued up, mill the parts for the stretcher systems that support the drawers. The front and back drawer stretchers are dovetailed to the case. The drawer runners are mortised into the stretchers. The runners are housed in shallow dadoes in the case sides and are cut ⅛ in. short and glued only at the front tenon to allow for seasonal movement of the case sides.

Because the molding around the top of the dresser is thicker than the top, I screw what is basically another drawer-stretcher assembly to the underside of the top to fill the gap. The front and back stretchers on this upper assembly don't need to be dovetailed to the case sides, and the runners are glued only at the front stretcher.

Attach the Molding

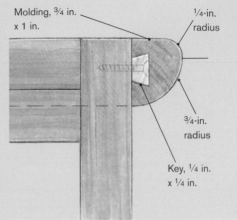

Molding, ³/₄ in. x 1 in.

¹/₄-in. radius

³/₄-in. radius

Key, ¹/₄ in. x ¹/₄ in.

THE FRONT MOLDING is glued on, but the side moldings are held in place with dovetailed keys. To position a key, insert it into the molding, leaving a few inches exposed at the front. Align the molding flush with the case top and screw the key to the case. Gradually slide the molding back, exposing more of the key.

SLIDE THE MOLDING INTO PLACE. After attaching the key, cut it apart at 3-in. intervals to allow the case to expand and contract with seasonal humidity changes. Apply glue at the front corner of the case and slide the molding onto the case from the back.

Dovetailing Lipped Drawer Fronts

BEGIN BY ROUTING A RABBET along the sides and top of the drawer front (1). After scribing the pins with a knife (2), remove the waste with a router equipped with a fence (3). A platform clamped to the benchtop makes it easy to secure the drawer front while routing. Then pare to the scribe line with a sharp chisel (4). After assembly, use a shoulder plane to trim the pins flush (5).

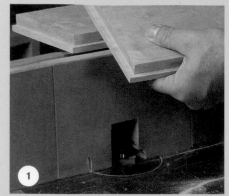

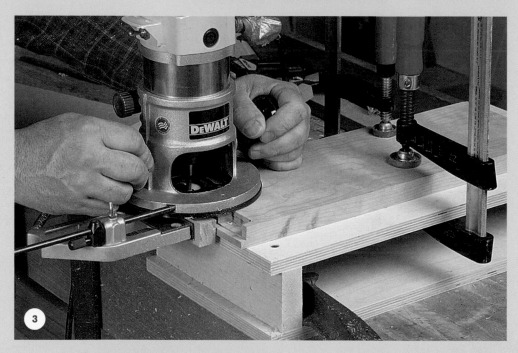

Molding and Base Require Dovetails

The molding is glued along the case front and attached with dovetail keys along the case sides to allow for wood movement. I learned this method from woodworker Christian Becksvoort. A dovetail slot is routed along the side moldings, and matching keys are screwed to the case side. The molding slides on from the rear and is glued only at the front corner.

The bracket base is dovetailed at the front with the upper portion of the joint mitered for a clean look. Run a rabbet along the top of the bracket base for setting in the carcase. Glue the carcase to the base along the front, and attach the base to the sides with screw blocks that are glued to the base and screwed to the carcase in elongated holes to allow for seasonal movement.

Size and Fit Lipped Drawer Fronts

The drawer fronts on this dresser are rabbeted along the top and sides to create a lip. This adds visual interest to the piece and does away with the need for stop blocks inside the case. However, it does make fitting and dovetailing the drawer a bit tougher.

Normally, when making drawers, I start with a snug fit and plane the sides until they fit the opening on the carcase. But the lipped front makes planing the sides difficult, so it's important to get the dimensions right the first time. I do this with the help of a story stick. Before making any cuts, be sure to note the widths and heights of all drawer openings and adjust your cut list accordingly.

Begin by ripping all of the drawer parts to width. The sides are ⅛ in. narrower than the height of the opening. The backs are ⅝ in. narrower than the opening, as they also must provide clearance for the drawer bottoms. The fronts are cut ⅛ in. wider than the height of the opening.

Next, crosscut all of the drawer parts to length. The sides are cut so that they reach just short of the case back. Size the drawer backs to fit snugly in the opening. The fronts are cut ½ in. longer than the drawer back. Once all of the pieces have been dimensioned, run a ¼-in.-wide by 9/16-in.-deep rabbet along the top and on the end of each drawer front. Don't profile the lipped edges yet.

Dovetail the drawer parts Now you are set to cut the dovetails for the drawer parts. Begin by cutting the tails on the drawer sides using the same tablesaw method used for the carcase. The through-dovetails on the drawer backs are straightforward. However, the half-blind dovetails on the drawer fronts pose a challenge. The rabbeted lip prohibits you from sawing the full length of the pins. Instead, scribe the pins with a knife and use a router equipped with a fence to remove the waste. Then use a chisel to pare to the scribe lines where the router bit can't reach.

Before assembling the drawers, you must run a groove along the inside bottom edges of the drawer sides and drawer fronts to accommodate the drawer bottoms. You also must trim 1/32 in. off the bottom edge of each drawer front with the jointer. This will allow you to do the final fit of the assembled drawers by trimming only the bottom edge of the drawer sides. Trimming also prevents the bottom of the drawer front from scraping the stretcher when closing the drawer.

Next, rout a thumbnail profile along all four edges of the drawer fronts using a

Dresser Construction

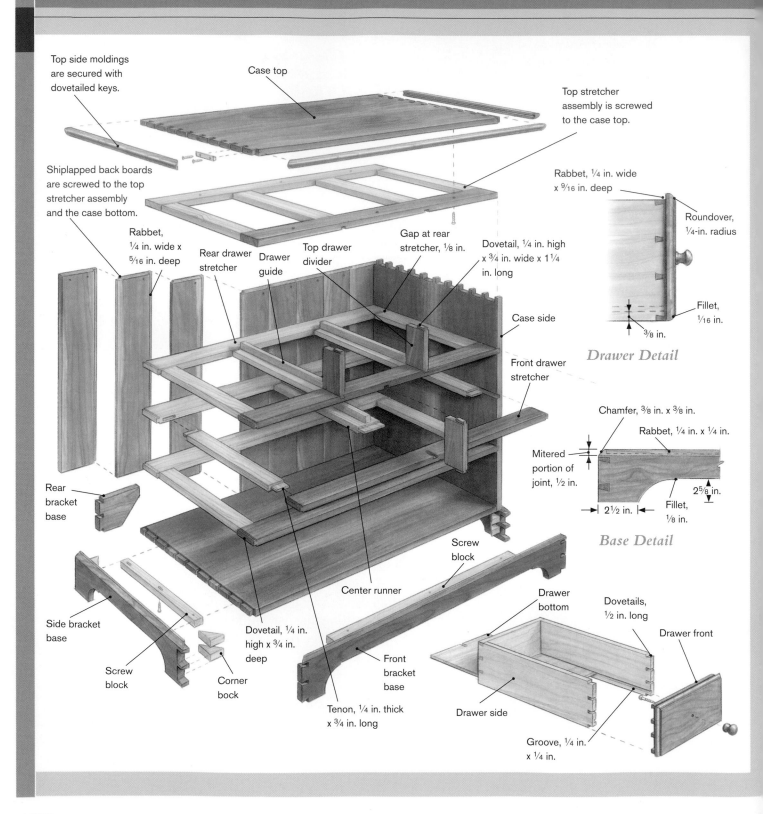

Top side moldings are secured with dovetailed keys.

Case top

Top stretcher assembly is screwed to the case top.

Shiplapped back boards are screwed to the top stretcher assembly and the case bottom.

Rabbet, 1/4 in. wide x 5/16 in. deep

Rear drawer stretcher

Drawer guide

Top drawer divider

Gap at rear stretcher, 1/8 in.

Dovetail, 1/4 in. high x 3/4 in. wide x 1 1/4 in. long

Case side

Front drawer stretcher

Rear bracket base

Side bracket base

Screw block

Corner bock

Dovetail, 1/4 in. high x 3/4 in. deep

Tenon, 1/4 in. thick x 3/4 in. long

Center runner

Screw block

Front bracket base

Drawer bottom

Drawer side

Groove, 1/4 in. x 1/4 in.

Dovetails, 1/2 in. long

Drawer front

Rabbet, 1/4 in. wide x 9/16 in. deep

Roundover, 1/4-in. radius

Fillet, 1/16 in.

3/8 in.

Drawer Detail

Chamfer, 3/8 in. x 3/8 in.

Rabbet, 1/4 in. x 1/4 in.

Mitered portion of joint, 1/2 in.

2 1/2 in.

Fillet, 1/8 in.

2 5/8 in.

Base Detail

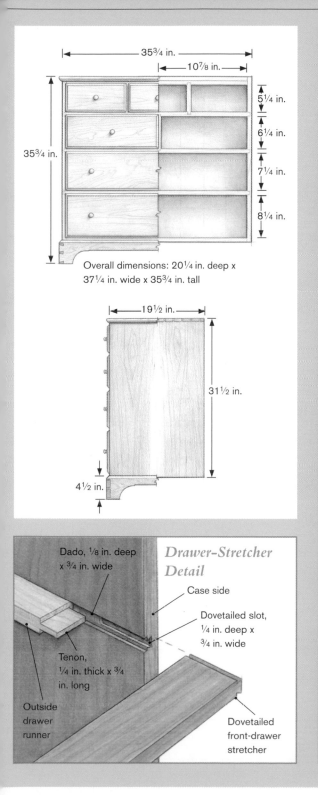

35³⁄₄ in.

10⁷⁄₈ in.

5¹⁄₄ in.

35³⁄₄ in.

6¹⁄₄ in.

7¹⁄₄ in.

8¹⁄₄ in.

Overall dimensions: 20¹⁄₄ in. deep x
37¹⁄₄ in. wide x 35³⁄₄ in. tall

19¹⁄₂ in.

31¹⁄₂ in.

4¹⁄₂ in.

Drawer-Stretcher Detail

Dado, ¹⁄₈ in. deep x ³⁄₄ in. wide

Case side

Dovetailed slot, ¹⁄₄ in. deep x ³⁄₄ in. wide

Tenon, ¹⁄₄ in. thick x ³⁄₄ in. long

Outside drawer runner

Dovetailed front-drawer stretcher

CUT LIST

WOOD	PART NAME	QUANTITY	DIMENSIONS
Cherry			
	Back boards	8	⁵⁄₈ x 4¹⁄₂ x 30³⁄₄
	Bracket base, front	1	³⁄₄ x 4¹⁄₂ x 36³⁄₄
	Bracket base, sides	2	³⁄₄ x 4¹⁄₂ x 20
	Case bottom	1	³⁄₄ x 18⁷⁄₈ x 35³⁄₈
	Case sides	2	³⁄₄ x 19¹⁄₂ x 31¹⁄₂
	Case top	1	³⁄₄ x 19¹⁄₂ x 35³⁄₄
	Drawer divider, second row	1	³⁄₄ x 2¹⁄₂ x 6³⁄₄
	Drawer dividers, top row	2	³⁄₄ x 2¹⁄₂ x 5³⁄₄
	Drawer fronts, top row	3	⁷⁄₈ x 5³⁄₈ x 11³⁄₈
	Drawer fronts, second row	2	⁷⁄₈ x 6³⁄₈ x 17¹⁄₄
	Drawer front, third row	1	⁷⁄₈ x 7³⁄₈ x 34³⁄₄
	Drawer front, bottom row	1	⁷⁄₈ x 8³⁄₈ x 34³⁄₄
	Drawer stretchers, front	3	³⁄₄ x 2¹⁄₂ x 35
	Molding, top front	1	³⁄₄ x 1 x 37¹⁄₄
	Moldings, top side	2	³⁄₄ x 1 x 20¹⁄₄
	Stretcher, top front	1	³⁄₄ x 2¹⁄₂ x 34¹⁄₄
Soft Maple			
	Bracket base, rear	2	³⁄₄ x 4¹⁄₄ x 6
	Drawer backs, top row	3	¹⁄₂ x 4¹⁄₂ x 10⁷⁄₈
	Drawer backs, second row	2	¹⁄₂ x 5¹⁄₂ x 16³⁄₄
	Drawer back, third row	1	¹⁄₂ x 6¹⁄₂ x 34¹⁄₄
	Drawer back, bottom row	1	¹⁄₂ x 7¹⁄₂ x 34¹⁄₄
	Drawer guides	3	³⁄₄ x 1 x 13³⁄₄
	Drawer sides, top row	6	¹⁄₂ x 5¹⁄₈ x 18
	Drawer sides, second row	4	¹⁄₂ x 6¹⁄₈ x 18
	Drawer sides, third row	2	¹⁄₂ x 7¹⁄₈ x 18
	Drawer sides, bottom row	2	¹⁄₂ x 8¹⁄₈ x 18
	Drawer stretchers, rear	3	³⁄₄ x 2¹⁄₂ x 35
	Runners, outside	8	³⁄₄ x 2 x 15¹⁄₄
	Runners, center	5	³⁄₄ x 3 x 15¹⁄₄
	Stretcher, top rear	1	³⁄₄ x 2¹⁄₂ x 34¹⁄₄
Pine			
	Drawer bottoms, top row	3	¹⁄₂ x 17³⁄₄ x 10³⁄₈
	Drawer bottoms, second row	2	¹⁄₂ x 17³⁄₄ x 16¹⁄₄
	Drawer bottom, third row	1	¹⁄₂ x 17³⁄₄ x 33³⁄₄
	Drawer bottom, bottom row	1	¹⁄₂ x 17³⁄₄ x 33³⁄₄
	Misc. screw and corner blocks		³⁄₄ in. thick

Sources

Irion Lumber Co.
P.O. Box 954
Wellsboro, PA 16901
570-724-1895
www.ironlumber.com

¼-in. roundover bit. Finally, glue up the parts and flush the front dovetails with a shoulder plane and the back dovetails with a block plane.

Turned knobs top off the drawers

Turned cherry knobs are available through catalog retailers. However, I turned my own to ensure that the wood color matched. Making them by hand also allowed me to graduate the size of the knobs to match the graduated drawers.

Oil Finish Highlights the Wood

I finished the dresser with Waterlox, a wipe-on oil-based finish. Wipe-on oil finishes are easy to apply, they don't mask the beauty of the wood, and they don't depend on a dust-free environment for application. The biggest key to success in using an oil finish is surface preparation. Many finishing experts will insist that sanding with an abrasive greater than 150 grit is a waste of time. I'm certainly not a finishing expert, and I'm no big fan of sanding, but I've learned that if I want a blotch-free oil finish, I have to sand to at least 400 grit before applying the first coat of oil.

Start by wiping on two heavy coats and letting each dry thoroughly, not worrying about raised grain or dust nibs. Apply a third coat and, with 600-grit sandpaper, sand the dresser while it's still wet; then wipe off the excess oil with a dry rag. After this coat has dried, apply two to four very thin coats of oil using a circular motion to work the oil into the surface, followed by long strokes with the grain. Finish by applying paste wax with steel wool. Buff with a soft cloth for a smooth, satin luster.

★*Please note price estimates are from 2004.*

MICHAEL PEKOVICH is *Fine Woodworking* magazine's art director and an avid furniture maker.

Building a Strong, Light Carcase

BY GARRETT HACK

Some people think that the larger a piece is, the more difficult it is to build. That's true to a certain extent, but designing and building smaller, more delicate pieces that still will stand up to the rigors of normal household life—kids and dogs included—is a challenge of its own. Perhaps the most difficult situation is the table or desk with drawers.

Three pieces of wood joined to form a U-shape have virtually no structural integrity. Exert a little pressure on one side, and the corner joint will fail. In contrast, if you join four pieces of wood to form a box, you've got a fairly sturdy structure. Put a top (or bottom) on the box, and you have a structure that will take some abuse. But if you cut a bunch of holes in the front of the piece (drawer openings), you've eliminated much of its strength.

Furniture makers have come up with various ways of strengthening desks and tables whose fronts are mostly drawers, such as beefing up the frame internally and using heavy-duty front rails. Neither of these is ideal. An internal frame (basically, a shallow box around the internal perimeter of the

SIMPLE LINES, REMARKABLE WOODS, and structural integrity combine with impeccable craftsmanship to make the author's Shaker-inspired hall table a jewel in wood. All drawer faces are from one pear board; the carcase is carefully grain- and figure-matched bird's-eye maple, and the pulls and pegs are rosewood.

ROSEWOOD PEGS STRENGTHEN THE JOINT, and they add a distinctive touch to the author's table. The adjustable wrench keeps the pegs properly oriented, parallel to the case's top and sides.

carcase, sometimes with a crossbar) reduces usable drawer space, and thick, bulky front rails may fit the bill structurally, but they aren't the most aesthetic solution. My solution addresses both of these shortcomings.

Unless you use it to stand on while changing a lightbulb, most of the stress on a piece of furniture like this is from racking, not downward compression. What's needed then are not massive front rails, but deep rails—rails that tie the front of the piece to the three solid sides of the carcase and provide maximum resistance to racking. Together with the table's leg-and-apron construction, these thin, deep rails ensure a piece of furniture that is tough but still looks quite refined, as shown in the photo on p. 105.

Carcase Joinery

After I've prepared all my stock and turned the legs for this side table, I begin cutting the joinery. I used a pair of haunched tenons for each leg-to-apron joint (see the drawing on the facing page). Adding a haunch to a tenon increases the glue area of the joint, making it stronger. Even more importantly, though, the haunches increase the mechanical resistance of the joint to twisting.

I lay out my mortises first, clamping all the legs together side by side so that the

mortises are all positioned identically. I make all of the mortises with a shop-built slot mortiser, but if you don't have a mortiser, a plunge router and mortising jig (or mortise chisel and mallet) will also work fine. Next I square the ends and then chop the haunch mortises with a sharp paring chisel. To keep the haunch mortises consistent, one to another, I make a small pattern from scrap, and use the pattern as a depth and angle check.

After I've cut all the leg mortises and the corresponding apron tenons, I cut, plane, and scrape the front rails. It's important that the faces of the rails that accept the stiles be finish-planed now so that you don't alter the fit by removing stock after cutting the joinery. I also cut the bead into the lower front rail and aprons now, using a scratch stock. I clamp the three front rails together edge to edge to align them, as I did the legs, and I mark out the tenons at each end and the dovetailed slots for the stiles.

I rout the dovetailed slots first, and then work out the pin width and depth on one end of each of the stiles, leaving them long so I can rout a few trial pins. Then, once I have a good pin, I cut the stiles to length and rout the remaining pins. Next I mortise the front legs for the rails, mortise the rails themselves for the drawer runner and kicker tenons, and then cut the front rail tenons (see the drawing on the facing page for joinery details).

Because I wanted maximum joint strength, I mitered the apron tenons at each rear leg. Mitering the tenons allows me to make them longer than would be possible if their ends were square, increasing the glue surface and strengthening the joint. I mark the cutoff line on the tenon by sticking a sharply tapered pencil in through the opposite mortise.

While the leg-to-apron joints are still together, I also score the legs where the

Shaker Side Table

Note: Measurements do not include tenon or dovetail lengths.

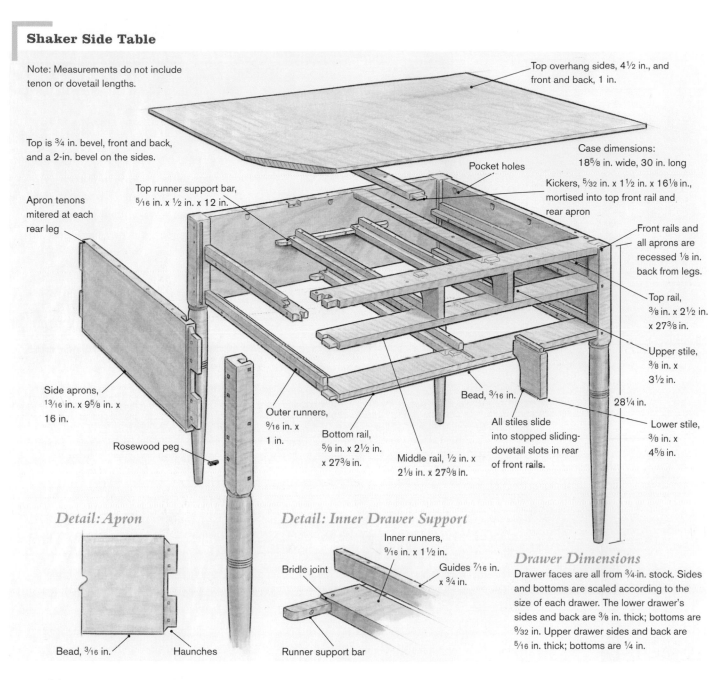

Top overhang sides, 4½ in., and front and back, 1 in.

Top is ¾ in. bevel, front and back, and a 2-in. bevel on the sides.

Pocket holes

Case dimensions: 18⅝ in. wide, 30 in. long

Kickers, 5/32 in. x 1½ in. x 16⅛ in., mortised into top front rail and rear apron

Apron tenons mitered at each rear leg

Top runner support bar, 5/16 in. x ½ in. x 12 in.

Front rails and all aprons are recessed ⅛ in. back from legs.

Top rail, ⅜ in. x 2½ in. x 27⅜ in.

Upper stile, ⅜ in. x 3½ in.

Side aprons, 13/16 in. x 9⅝ in. x 16 in.

Rosewood peg

Outer runners, 9/16 in. x 1 in.

Bottom rail, ⅝ in. x 2½ in. x 27⅜ in.

Middle rail, ½ in. x 2⅛ in. x 27⅞ in.

Bead, 3/16 in.

All stiles slide into stopped sliding-dovetail slots in rear of front rails.

28¼ in.

Lower stile, ⅜ in. x 4⅝ in.

Detail: Apron

Bead, 3/16 in.

Haunches

Detail: Inner Drawer Support

Inner runners, 9/16 in. x 1½ in.

Bridle joint

Guides 7/16 in. x ¾ in.

Runner support bar

Drawer Dimensions

Drawer faces are all from ¾-in. stock. Sides and bottoms are scaled according to the size of each drawer. The lower drawer's sides and back are ⅜ in. thick; bottoms are 9/32 in. Upper drawer sides and back are 5/16 in. thick; bottoms are ¼ in.

tops of the aprons intersect them and carry these marks around each leg with a sharp knife. I crosscut the legs just shy of this mark. Then I plane the legs level with the rest of the carcase after glue-up so that legs and aprons are all precisely even.

I drill the pocket holes in the aprons, using an angled fixture on my drill press to hold the apron in place. I use a Forstner bit first to provide a flat seat for the screw head and then follow with a slightly oversized

twist bit to allow for seasonal movement of the wood. I generally prefer buttons for attaching tabletops, but for this small a table, either the buttons would have to be so thin that they would have broken, or they would have to be so thick that they would have interfered with the drawers.

Assembly

After I finish planing and scraping all parts not already smoothed, I begin the assembly:

Building and Fitting Drawers

The trick to getting drawers to fit sweetly is to cut the faces to fit the openings exactly (see the left photo on the facing page). If you can't fit a drawer in its opening, you can always plane the sides to fit–but you can't add any wood back if you start with a sloppy fit.

I cut and pare the dovetail pins on the drawer face first. Then I finish-plane the inside and outside of the drawer faces so that they are at final thickness before I mark and cut the tails at the front of the drawer sides. I also drill the holes for the tenon on the pull now.

To keep the drawers both strong and light, I varied the drawer side thickness, so the smaller upper drawers have thinner sides than those below. As with the drawer faces, I finish-plane the insides and outsides of the drawer sides before marking out the tails, except for the first few inches of the outside face around the joint. I leave this area unplaned at this stage because I'll be cleaning up the joint with my plane after glue-up anyway.

Once I've cut and test-fitted the drawer-face dovetails, I cut the sides to length and rout sliding dovetail slots from the bottom of the sides about ¾ in. in from the end.

Because the thickness of the drawer back won't affect the fit of the sliding dovetail joint, I finish-plane the backs after I have fit the joint.

I used the tablesaw to plow drawer bottom grooves into the faces and sides. I also set aside a piece of scrap with the groove in it to use later for sizing the beveled drawer bottoms.

Beginning with the face dovetails, I assemble each drawer, squaring each corner as I tap it home and clamping the joint if necessary to keep it square. Often I won't even use clamps, though, because a properly fitting set of dovetails doesn't require clamping. After I've joined the drawer face and sides, I slide the back into its dovetailed slot in the side. When the back is two-thirds home, I put a small amount of glue in the slot and on the pin and finish tapping it home. Then I check (and adjust, if necessary) again for square by measuring the diagonals and comparing. I set the drawer on my tablesaw's flat-ground top while the glue is setting up. This way, twist won't be built into the drawer from sitting on a less-than-flat surface.

I proportioned the thickness of the drawer bottom to the drawer sides by eye and by feel: thinner bottoms for the smaller upper drawers and thicker bottoms for the larger drawers below. I beveled the underside of the drawer bottoms, so I could keep the bottom thicker in the middle (and therefore stronger). And I could position the bottom a little deeper in the drawer and still have enough lip to support the bottom securely.

first both rear legs and apron, and then the two front legs and two bottom drawer rails. After the glue has set on these first two sub–assemblies, I join them with the side aprons.

The top drawer rail finishes the case assembly (see the drawing on p. 107). This rail was sometimes left out by the Shakers in similar pieces, but it's an important element when trying to maximize strength while retaining a delicate-looking carcase.

Not only does it add strength to the carcase, but it also completes the drawer face frame visually and drops the top drawers slightly so that they're more accessible beneath the overhang.

I cut the dovetailed ends of the rail first, lay it in position, scribe around it, and chop the mortise to receive it. Then I drill and countersink a few holes in the rail to secure the top and glue and screw (for insurance)

DRAWER FACE BLANKS THAT ARE SNUG BUT DO NOT BIND are key to sweetly fitting drawers. Hack leaves the drawers snug at this point, so there will be a minimum amount of play when he planes the sides.

PLANING DRAWER SIDES TO FIT IS A PAINS-TAKING PROCESS. Hack takes a few passes with a plane and checks the drawer in its opening. The chamois between the drawer side and the board supporting it protects the inside face of the drawer side.

Also, a beveled bottom has a certain elegance. I glue up the bottoms from thicknessed stock, rip and crosscut each bottom to size, finish-plane the top surface, and then rough out the bevels on the tablesaw. Then I plane each bevel until it fits in the grooved piece of scrap I saved for testing this fit, finish-plane the underside of the bottom, and slide it home into the drawer frame, securing it with two screws at one-third points across the bottom into the drawer back.

The first step in fitting drawers is to plane the area I left unplaned around the half-blind dovetails joining the drawer faces to the sides. Then I just plane both sides equally, constantly testing the drawer in the opening until there is a total

of about $\frac{1}{16}$-in. play from side to side, as shown in the photo above right. (For larger drawers, I'd leave a bit more clearance.)

Next, I level the bottom of the sides and face with a jointer plane, working with the grain all the way around. I also ease all the edges, so they're more pleasing visually and tactilely and to help the drawers glide more smoothly. Once the bottom is level, I flip the drawer over and level the top, stopping often to check the drawer's fit. For drawers of this size, $\frac{1}{16}$-in. play at the top is plenty for seasonal movement.

the rail into place. I level the top of the case with a jointer plane, working slowly around the piece and taking care not to tear out any fibers as I pass over the legs. I finish the carcase assembly by tapping the stiles home into the stopped sliding dovetail slots in the front rails, dabbing just a bit of glue into the slots.

I pin all the joints with small, square rosewood pegs because they add mechanical

strength to the joints and because I like the contrast with the maple. I mark out peg locations with an awl, rub a small square of masking tape over the hole-to-be (it prevents tearout when drilling), and drill my holes. To make it easier to fit the pegs into their holes, I square the top third of each hole roughly with a paring chisel, pare the bottom two-thirds of each peg fairly round, and taper the end of each peg with a little pencil sharpener. I drive the pegs home with a 12-oz. hammer (rosewood is very dense and not likely to be damaged by the metal). When hammering, I hold onto the pegs with a small adjustable wrench to keep the pegs parallel to top and sides (see the photo on p. 106). I tap the pegs home and then pare them almost flush with a chisel, finishing up with a block plane and a scraper.

The next step is to install the web frame: drawer runners, guides, and kickers. If you want the drawers to glide smoothly, you must plane all wear surfaces glassy smooth (wax applied later will further reduce friction). The guides should be parallel to the carcase sides and the runners flush with the top of the drawer rails. I cut the guides so they're just shy of the stile faces and the rear of the carcase; that way, I only have to worry about the fit of the runners.

The runners for the top bay of drawers serve as kickers for the bottom drawers, preventing them from dropping down when they're partially open (see the drawing for details). I thickness the runner stock so that it's ⅛ in. thinner than the front rails, which allows the drawer to drop slightly but not scrape the kicker on opening. I thickness the top drawer kickers similarly.

I glue and screw the outside runners and guides into place. For the interior runners, I tenon the front end to slip into the mortises in the face-frame rails, and then I use a bridle joint at the rear to attach the runners to the support bars, as shown in the drawing on p. 107. The beauty of using this bridle joint is that it allows adjustment of the runners horizontally and vertically before screwing the bar in, and it lets me install the runners and guides after the case is assembled, making that job considerably simpler.

I center the guides on the runners, apply glue, and screw through the runners into the guides from below. Winding sticks help me get everything on the same plane, and a few sticks cut to exactly the widths of the drawer openings keep the guides parallel. The last parts to go in are the top drawer kickers, which I tenon into the top drawer rail at the front and set into a mortise at the top of the apron in the back. In addition to keeping the drawers from dropping when they're opened, the kickers also add to the overall integrity of the carcase.

I like to have the top and case completed and assembled before starting on drawers in case there's any tension between the carcase and top. I don't want any surprises (drawers binding, for example) after I've fitted the drawers (see the sidebar on pp. 108–109 for how I build and fit drawers). I milled the boards for the top nearly to final thickness, matched and glued them, and then finish-planed and scraped top and bottom.

I beveled the underside of the top all around, rough-cutting the bevel on the tablesaw and then finishing up with a sharp plane held askew. I drew a pencil line all around the edge as a guide for the bevel. This thin beveled edge is pleasant visually, lightening the top in appearance, but without diminishing the mass and the strength of the top in the middle. Before securing the top, I apply a coat of finish to both the top and bottom.

The finish is built up of thin coats of spar varnish, linseed oil, and turpentine. I rub each coat in well, let it dry until it just starts to tack up, and then vigorously rub off any excess. To bring out the contrasting grain of the bird's eyes, I add a small amount of Minwax Golden Oak oil stain to the varnish mixture. After three or four coats of this finish, inside and out, I polish the whole piece with steel wool and a mixture of beeswax, linseed oil, and turpentine. I give the drawer runners, guides, and bearing surfaces of the drawer sides the same treatment.

GARRETT HACK is a furniture designer, maker, and one-horse farmer in Thetford Center, Vermont.

A Small Bureau
Built to Last

The dovetail joint's prevalence and persistence is due to its unsurpassed ability to hold pieces of wood together. The painted chest of drawers I made (see the photo below) illustrates the strength and versatility of the dovetail in a variety of forms. Tapered sliding half-dovetails lock the top to the sides;

half-blind dovetails join the sides to the bottom; sliding dovetails link the drawer dividers to the sides; and through- and half-blind dovetails join the drawers (see the drawings on pp. 113 and 114).

All this dovetailing makes the piece rock solid, but it is hidden strength. The chest has an unimposing scale that suits it to a

BY ROBERT TREANOR

DOVETAILS HIDE BEHIND MOLDINGS AND PAINT. This sofa-side chest of drawers packs a robust array of joinery in a small frame.

TAPERED SOCKET IN TWO STEPS. First rout dadoes along the taper lines, as at right in the photo above. Then switch to a dovetail bit, clamp the fence parallel to the square layout line, and cut the dovetailed side of the sockets, as at left in the photo above.

SLIDING HALF-DOVETAILS ARE FINISHED with a rabbet plane. Cutting the taper of a sliding half-dovetail square with a rabbet plane instead of sloped on both sides like a full sliding dovetail makes a joint that's easier to fit. Stop and check the fit frequently as you approach the taper depth line.

PERFECTING HALF-BLIND DOVETAILS. After clearing waste with a Forstner bit in the drill press, the author pares to the lap line between pins of the half-blind dovetails at the bottom of the carcase sides. The board clamped to the workpiece guides the chisel for chopping through end grain.

living room, where it could stand at the end of a sofa and serve as an end table as well as a bureau. The moldings that hide its joinery are clean and simple, particularly the single-arch molding on the front of the chest with its bird's-mouth joints at the drawer dividers and its tapers, top and bottom.

Construction

I began the chest by gluing up material to form the top, bottom, and sides. I used ash, a ring-porous, coarse-textured hardwood. Because I intended to paint the piece, I wasn't too careful about the color match of planks. But because the wood's coarse texture would show, I took pains to ensure figure and grain were consistent between the boards to be edge-glued.

A strong, self-locking joint I used tapered, sliding half-dovetails to join the case sides to the top (see the drawing detail on the facing page). This joint is excellent in a situation where one case member runs past or overhangs another. Its advantages are many: It is self-locking, so it will hold both pieces rigid and flat even if the glue should fail; it won't bind in assembly; and it is strong. The half-dovetail is a variation on tapered sliding dovetails in which the pin seen in cross section has only one wedged side; the other side is simply a rabbet that tapers from one end of the joint to the other.

I made sockets for these pins in two stages. The first cut was a dado routed with a ⅜-in. straight bit along the tapered layout line. I routed the dado to a depth of ½ in. in several passes. With both dadoes cut, I changed to a ½-in. dovetail bit, set my scrap-stock fence parallel to the square layout line, and routed the dovetail side of the socket in one pass (see the top photo at left).

I kept the dovetail bit at the same setting to cut the mating tapered half-dovetail

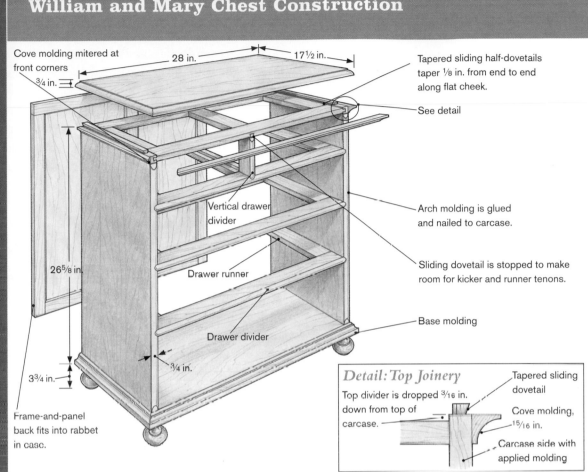

William and Mary Chest Construction

Cove molding mitered at front corners

¾ in.

28 in.

17½ in.

Tapered sliding half-dovetails taper ⅛ in. from end to end along flat cheek.

See detail

Vertical drawer divider

26⅝ in.

Drawer runner

Arch molding is glued and nailed to carcase.

Sliding dovetail is stopped to make room for kicker and runner tenons.

Drawer divider

Base molding

3¾ in.

¾ in.

Frame-and-panel back fits into rabbet in case.

Detail: Top Joinery

Top divider is dropped ³⁄₁₆ in. down from top of carcase.

Tapered sliding dovetail

Cove molding, ¹⁵⁄₁₆ in.

Carcase side with applied molding

pins on the tops of the case sides. I locked the side in my bench vise and clamped a freshly milled piece of scrap along the top edge to give the router a greater bearing surface. Then, using the router's guide fence, I cut the dovetail along the outside face of the sides. Next I cut the tapered side of the half-dovetail with a rabbet plane. I clamped a fence along the shoulder line and guided the plane against it, as shown in the center photo on the facing page. I planed down close to the taper line, taking light passes as I neared it. Before I reached the line, I started trial-fitting the joint. This type of joint goes together sloppily until it's nearly home. The final inch or so will require firm hand pres-

sure or even light mallet blows to close the joint completely. If you plane off too much, you can glue shims along the tapered edge and plane again to fit.

Half-blind dovetails These join the case sides to the bottom. I waited before cutting the bottom to length until I had the sides dry-fit to the top and could get an empirical measurement. I used nine tails across the width of the bottom, but the number or spacing isn't critical.

Because the pins on half-blind dovetails don't go through, it's harder to use them to lay out the tails, so I cut the tails first and lay out the pins from them. I do most of

Corner Joinery

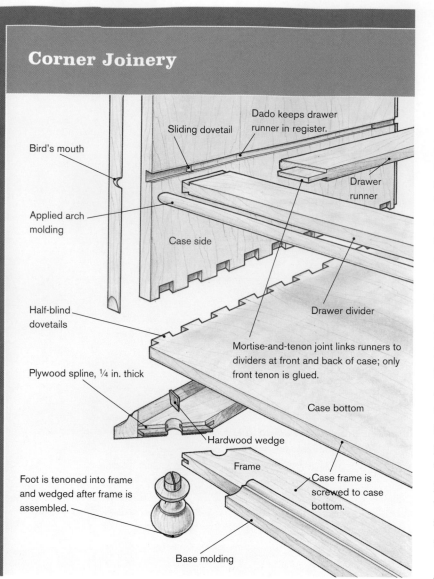

Bird's mouth

Sliding dovetail

Dado keeps drawer runner in register.

Applied arch molding

Drawer runner

Case side

Half-blind dovetails

Drawer divider

Mortise-and-tenon joint links runners to dividers at front and back of case; only front tenon is glued.

Plywood spline, ¼ in. thick

Case bottom

Hardwood wedge

Frame

Foot is tenoned into frame and wedged after frame is assembled.

Case frame is screwed to case bottom.

Base molding

my dovetail sawing with Japanese dozuki saws, which are fast, accurate, easy to control, and leave only a hairline kerf. After using the tails to lay out the pins in the sides, I cut and chop the remainder of the joint. I often hog out waste between the pins with a Forstner bit in the drill press. That makes the chisel work much lighter (see the bottom photo on p. 112). These joints won't show, but the more accurately they're cut, the stronger the case will be and the closer the case will be to self-squaring. The joints will also provide practice, if needed, for the half-blind dovetails

at the fronts of the drawers, the first place many people look when they open a drawer.

Dividers and tenons The joinery for the drawer dividers at the front and back of the case and the runners between them is a hybrid. The dividers are attached to the sides with sliding dovetails, which keep the sides from bowing and the dividers in place. The runners are tongued along one edge and let into a dado in the cabinet side and are tenoned at each end into the drawer dividers (see the drawing at left).

I cut a ½-in.-wide dado ⅛ in. deep for each of the runners and for the kickers above the top drawers. As well as housing the runners, the dadoes index the router jig I use to cut the sliding dovetail sockets for the dividers. The jig is a simple assembly: An indexing bar on its underside fits in the dado, arms guide the router, and a center section both limits the router's travel and provides a place to attach the jig to the workpiece with drywall screws (see the top photo on p. 116). With the jig in place, I waste the bulk of the material with a ½-in. straight bit. Then the socket can be cut in one pass with a ¾-in. dovetail bit.

With the drawer dividers cut to length, scraped, and sanded, I cut dovetails on their ends. I cut them on the router table with the same bit I used to cut their mating dovetail sockets. I clamp a high fence to the table to aid in keeping the pieces stable and run them past the bit vertically. The remaining joinery on the dividers are mortises cut at each end that will receive the tenons on the runners. I rout these with the dividers wedge-locked in a mortising box. I use a plunge router with a straight bit and cut in several passes. Then I square up the mortises by hand.

To fit the runners, I cut a ⅛-in. by ½-in. tongue on one edge and tenons on each end. When the case is assembled, I'll glue the tenons into the front dividers but will leave them dry at the back to allow for seasonal movement of the case. Be sure to leave a gap between the shoulder of the dry tenon and the back divider. The size of the gap will depend on what fluctuations of humidity the piece is likely to encounter.

Gluing Up the Case

The case is now nearly ready to glue up. But before that step, I shaped the edge of the top and routed rabbets in the parts to accept the frame-and-panel back. Because the joinery is all dovetails, I needed very few clamps. I used urea formaldehyde glue because it has a longer open time than the polyvinyl acetates (PVAs), and I planned to assemble the whole main case at once.

I began the assembly by applying glue to the tapered sliding half-dovetail sockets in the underside of the top. If the joint is a tight fit, only a small amount of glue is needed. I carefully slid the joint together, tapping lightly as needed. With the sides joined to the top, I turned the case upside down and glued the bottom to the sides, knocking the joints home evenly with a mallet and a block of scrap. Then I checked for square and cleaned off glue squeeze-out. If necessary, I use bar clamps to square up the case and hold things in alignment as the assembly continues.

I glued in the front dividers next, using glue judiciously and checking for square after each divider was glued in. Then I flipped the case over, so it sat on its front face. I applied glue to the mortises in the front dividers and installed the runners into the mortises and the dadoes cut into the sides, taking care not to get any glue in the dadoes. Finally, I glued the back dividers into their dovetail slots, pinching myself to refrain from gluing the mortise-and-tenon joint that attaches them to the runners.

Dressing the Case

To make the arch molding that covers the front edges of the case, I milled a straight-

PAINT PRONOUNCES THE TEXTURE. On a coarse-textured wood like ash, an opaque finish brings out the grain while hiding the color. The author left the ash case and drawer fronts unprimed to keep from filling the pores. He used painter's tape to mask the drawer sides and drawer openings. The interior finish is shellac.

grained board to ¾ in. thick. I cut the profile on a router table with a fingernail or half-radius bit. The entire edge is shaped, so I put several layers of masking tape along the outfeed side of the fence to create an offset bearing surface. I ripped the molded edges off the board with the tablesaw.

I applied the arch molding after the cove molding at the top of the case was already in place. Fitting the small bird's-mouth junctions of the arch moldings requires patience and sharp tools. I began by cutting the vertical pieces of molding to length and taping them to the front edge of the sides. Then I carefully marked the locations of the drawer dividers on the moldings, removed the moldings, and laid out the bird's mouths on their back faces. I cut the waste away with a fine-toothed backsaw and cleaned the cut by paring the remaining material with a sharp chisel, working up to the line with light cuts. Then I taped the moldings back onto the case and took measurements for horizontal moldings. I cut the horizontal moldings to length with a backsaw and a miter box. I glued and nailed the moldings to the case after all the joints had been fitted. I scarfed the ends of the moldings to meet the cove molding at the top

Sources

Primrose Distributing
54445 Rose Rd.
South Bend, IN 46628
219-234-6728

Horton Brasses
49 Nooks Hill Rd.
Cromwell, CT 06416
800-754-9127
www.horton-brasses.com

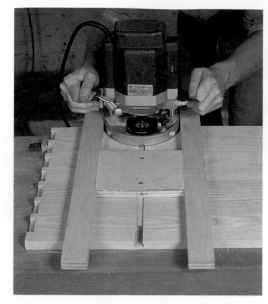

A GOOD JIG IS EASY TO LOCATE. The drawer-runner dadoes across the case sides double as an indexing slot for the simple router jig, which cuts the stopped sliding dovetail sockets for the drawer dividers.

of the case and the frame molding at the bottom. It's a small detail, but one that gives the piece its feeling of simple refinement. I made the cut by eye with a chisel, as shown in the photo below.

A painted finish is in keeping with the early 18th-century origins of this chest of drawers. I like the finish for the bold field of color it provides from afar and for the way it emphasizes the texture of the wood when seen up close. I used Fancy Chair Green, a latex finish that simulates milk paint, one of the Williamsburg Paint Colors made by the Stulb Co.; I bought mine from Primrose Distributing (see "Sources," at left). To prepare for painting, I wet down the surface with a damp rag to raise the grain. When the case was dry, I scuff-sanded the whiskers that had been raised. On the drawers, I put strips of painter's masking tape just behind the lap of the half-blind dovetails, creating the detail shown in the photo on p. 115. I applied the paint with a natural-bristle brush directly to the bare wood. I skipped a primer coat because I wanted to avoid filling the grain. I let the first coat dry overnight and rubbed down the surface with 0000 steel wool.

When a second coat had dried completely, I finished the case with a coat of satin varnish to make the color richer and to give the surface more depth. I finished the drawers and the inside of the case with three coats of a thinned shellac. Shellac cannot be used as a topcoat on the painted surfaces because it tends to lift the paint. With the finish completely dry, I mounted the period brass pulls (available from Horton Brasses, see "Sources"), glued and wedged the feet to the base frame, and screwed the base frame to the case.

ROBERT TREANOR, a former teacher in the woodworking program at San Francisco State University, builds and writes about furniture in the Bay area.

SCARFS CUT BY EYE. A few mallet taps produce the scarf detail at the ends of the vertical arch moldings. The author keeps his first scarf in view and approximates the angle on the other cuts.

Shaker Sewing Stand Remains Stylish, Practical

BY ROBERT TREANOR

Shaker sewing stands have a simplicity and a charm that few other pieces of furniture can match. Although I don't sew, and have buttonless shirts to prove it, I am drawn to these small stands. And that's not just because I like Shaker furniture. The stand's convenient size and two-way drawer (see the top drawing on p. 118) make it useful for any household—as an end table, a night stand, or especially as a hall table. Because the table is small, it will fit in almost any entryway, providing a place to drop the mail and your keys.

Most of us are familiar with the Shaker candle stands that have round tops. In Shaker communities, round stands were great for candles, but their tops didn't hold much else. Shaker craftsmen sometimes substituted rectangular tops for the round ones and suspended a drawer or two under the top to provide additional storage. These tripod stands usually are called sewing stands, although their main purpose is debatable.

Several versions of sewing stands with under-slung drawers evolved (see the sidebar on p. 120). The style I like best has a single drawer and cabriole-style (snake) legs, as shown in the photo at right. I built this stand mostly from cherry, with a few pine parts. Similar stands are attributed to the Hancock Shaker community in western Massachusetts and are, arguably, the most elegant. The height usually is about 26 in.

The legs on the original stand, on which my piece is based, are tenoned into the turned pedestal (a common feature of Hancock stands). The legs on my stand are joined to the pedestal by sliding dovetails. This joinery adds strength to the piece. Some original stands were built this way, and to further strengthen the connection, a metal plate (known as a spider) was secured to the bottom of the pedestal. I omitted the spider on my stand. The bottom drawing on p. 118 shows the patterns for the legs and the pedestal. I cut the leg dovetails on a router table. For the pedestal grooves, I use a jig and a handheld router with the pedestal still mounted

A TWO-WAY DRAWER hangs beneath this rectangular top.

Shaker-Stand Anatomy

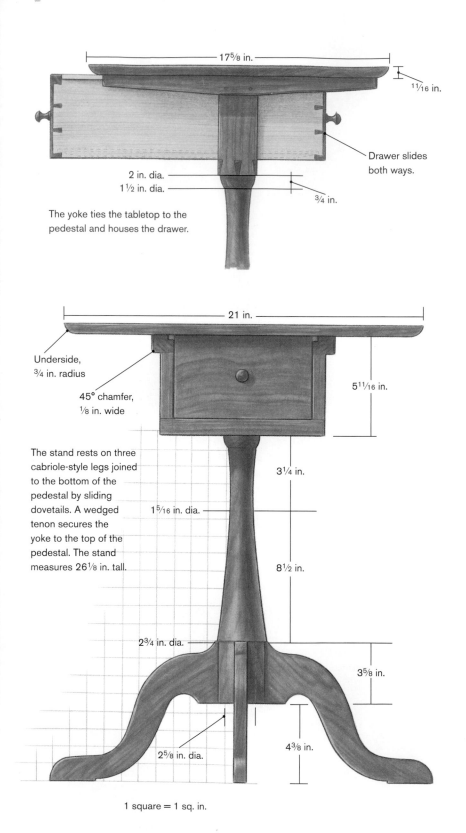

17⅝ in.

11⁄16 in.

Drawer slides
both ways.

2 in. dia.
1½ in. dia.

¾ in.

The yoke ties the tabletop to the
pedestal and houses the drawer.

21 in.

Underside,
¾ in. radius

45° chamfer,
⅛ in. wide

5¹¹⁄16 in.

The stand rests on three
cabriole-style legs joined
to the bottom of the
pedestal by sliding
dovetails. A wedged
tenon secures the
yoke to the top of the
pedestal. The stand
measures 26⅛ in. tall.

1⁵⁄16 in. dia.

3¼ in.

8½ in.

2¾ in. dia.

3⅝ in.

2⅝ in. dia.

4⅜ in.

1 square = 1 sq. in.

on the lathe, as shown in the bottom photo
on the facing page.

The Yoke Unites the Top, the Drawer, and the Pedestal

The tabletop on my stand is 21 in. wide
by 17⅝ in., front to back. I edge-joined
the top from two 4/4 boards. After glue-
up, I planed the top to 11⁄16 in. thick, and I
shaped the edges all around using a ¾-in.
roundover bit in my router. The radius is
clipped because of the table thickness, but
this slightly flattened round is intentional.

The U-shaped yoke that houses the
drawer and attaches the top to the base
distinguishes this stand from those with
two drawers. The two vertical members of
the yoke are joined to the crosspiece with
through dovetails. The yoke could be joined
with a single dovetail, but the original stand
had twin dovetails. I used one in the middle
and a half pin at each end.

**Dovetailing the crosspiece to the
uprights** I laid out the dovetail pins on the
horizontal crosspiece. For accuracy, I cut
the pins with a dozuki (a Japanese crosscut
saw) and a chisel. When I chopped out the
waste at the deep part of the pins, I guided
the chisel against a square block clamped to
the top of the work (see the top photo on
the facing page).

I lay out the tails on the uprights of
the yoke using the pins as a pattern. Just as
with the pins, I carefully saw the tails and
chop out the waste. Ideally, the joint will fit
right from the saw. But a little paring with a
chisel is often needed.

Tenoning the yoke to the pedestal The
yoke crosspiece is attached to the stand's
base by a turned tenon on top of the pedestal. I sized the tenon while the pedestal
was still on the lathe. I like to rough out the
tenon diameter so it's slightly greater than
the finished one. Then, using a gouge (you
could also use a skew), I slowly trimmed

Yoke and Drawer Supports

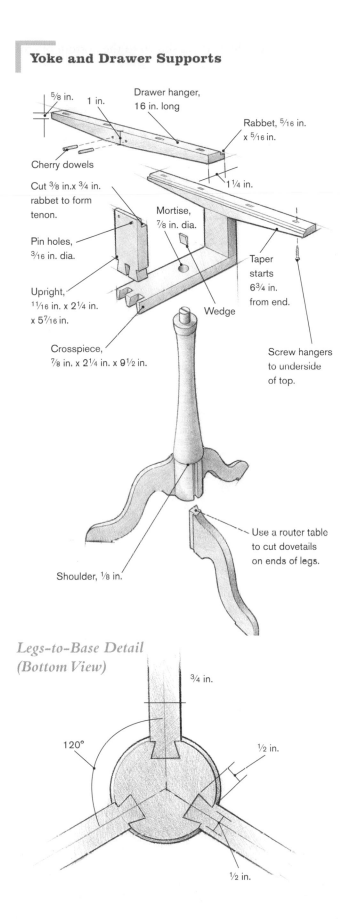

5/8 in.

1 in.

Drawer hanger, 16 in. long

Rabbet, 5/16 in. x 5/16 in.

Cherry dowels

Cut 3/8 in. x 3/4 in. rabbet to form tenon.

Pin holes, 3/16 in. dia.

1 1/4 in.

Mortise, 7/8 in. dia.

Upright, 11/16 in. x 2 1/4 in. x 5 7/16 in.

Wedge

Crosspiece, 7/8 in. x 2 1/4 in. x 9 1/2 in.

Taper starts 6 3/4 in. from end.

Screw hangers to underside of top.

Use a router table to cut dovetails on ends of legs.

Shoulder, 1/8 in.

Legs-to-Base Detail
(Bottom View)

3/4 in.

120°

1/2 in.

1/2 in.

A GUIDE BLOCK IMPROVES ACCURACY. When chopping the through dovetails in the crosspiece, the author uses a block of wood to guide his chisel. The crosspiece forms the bottom of the U-shaped yoke.

GLUE AND INSERT A WEDGE in the slotted tenon to secure the yoke to the pedestal. Orient the wedge perpendicular to the crosspiece's grain to prevent splitting.

ROUTER JIG CUTS SLIDING DOVETAIL SOCKETS. With the pedestal still mounted on the lathe, use a router to cut sockets for the leg dovetails.

Stands Change Along With Shakers

BY JOHN KASSAY

The sewing stand gracefully expresses the Shaker principles of economy, utility, and order. Economy is reflected in the small amount of wood needed to make one. Utility and order are evident if you consider that the stands were used for sewing and other occupations of Shaker community sisters. The stands can be moved easily, and those with two drawers can accommodate two sewers.

There were several versions of the Shaker sewing stand (see the photo below). The differences are mostly due to regional and cultural influences. Knowing a bit of Shaker furniture history helps explain how the differences came to be.

Furniture styles driven by religion and work ethics: Shaker furniture passed through three somewhat distinct stylistic periods. The first is the Primitive period (about 1790 to 1820). It is marked by furniture that usually is heavy and plain in form, crudely made, but strong and functional.

In the Classic period (about 1820 to 1860), the pieces show greater utility, simplicity, and perfection—all attributable to spiritual inspiration, dedication to the Shaker community, and skill. This was the golden age of Shaker furniture making.

Victorian Shaker pieces, the most recent, have more decoration, such as moldings,

AMERICA'S SHAKER ERA. Robert Treanor reproduced the tables below (from left): an early peg-leg stand, a Classic-period stand, and a two-drawer stand (original shown above), the most modern of the three.

ornate turnings, contrasting woods, and fancy, commercially made pulls. These ornate elements were used to lure new members after the Civil War.

Variations on a stand: The earliest sewing stands probably had one drawer. One of the oldest stands I measured had a pedestal with three peg legs at the bottom and a turned transitional element on top, just below the drawer case. Stands with a single drawer surrounded by a yoke likely came shortly thereafter. They may or may not have Queen Anne (serpentine-style) legs, like the one shown in preceding pages.

The most recent sewing stands often have two drawers suspended from the tabletop. Cleats on the upper sides of the drawers slide in hangers. The hangers, attached to the table's underside, help retain flatness in the top. Many of these later stands had three Sheraton-style legs that give an umbrella shape to the base (see the photo at left). These two-drawer sewing stands are especially popular in America and are eagerly sought by antique-furniture collectors. Like most single-drawer stands, the two-drawer variety can be opened from the back.

JOHN KASSAY is a retired industrial arts teacher living in San Bruno, California. He's the author of *The Book of Shaker Furniture* (The University of Massachusetts Press, 1980) and a book (by the same press) titled *The Book of American Windsor Furniture: Styles and Techniques,* 1998.

the tenon down to size, stopping the lathe frequently and checking the tenon diameter with a dial caliper.

I bored the hole in the crosspiece and sawed a slot in the tenon before the yoke was assembled. Then I assembled the yoke, placed it on the pedestal, and drove a wedge, wet with glue, into the tenon to lock the yoke in place (see the center photo on p. 119). To avoid splitting the crosspiece, I oriented the wedge perpendicular to the grain.

The Drawer Is Suspended and Guided by Two Hangers

A ¼-in. by ¾-in. runner was glued and nailed to the top of each drawer side. The runners guide the drawer in two L-shaped hangers that connect the yoke and tabletop. The hangers, tapered gently at each end, have rabbets cut in the upper inside edges to support the drawer. Each hanger is attached to the underside of the top with four screws. I counterbored the slotted holes in the hangers to recess the round screw heads. To break the hard edges of the hangers, I used a spokeshave to make a ⅛-in., 45° chamfer around the outside.

The uprights are joined to the center of the hangers with pinned tenons (see the top drawing on p. 119). It's best to cut the tenons before you dovetail the other ends of the uprights. The stand that inspired mine has two pins at each juncture, which suggests that double tenons were used. I used single tenons, but I matched the look by pinning each tenon with two 3/16-in. cherry dowels.

I joined the drawer sides and fronts using half-blind dovetails. The original stand's drawer had through-dovetailed corners, but I opted for half-blind dovetails because I think their functional, understated look goes better with the nature of this stand. The drawer bottom is let into a groove all around the inside, frame-and-panel fashion (see the photo above). The

ASSEMBLE THE DRAWER WITH THE BEVEL DOWN. The pine bottom floats in grooves in the pine sides and in the cherry drawer fronts.

Drawer Detail

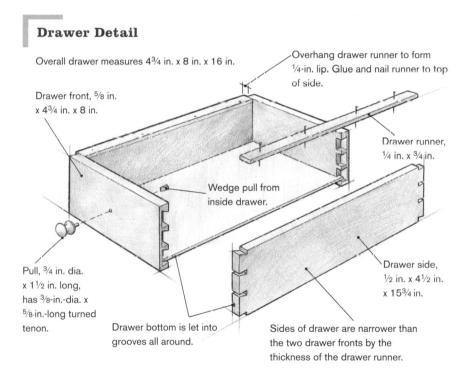

Overall drawer measures 4¾ in. x 8 in. x 16 in.

Drawer front, ⅝ in. x 4¾ in. x 8 in.

Overhang drawer runner to form ¼-in. lip. Glue and nail runner to top of side.

Drawer runner, ¼ in. x ¾ in.

Wedge pull from inside drawer.

Pull, ¾ in. dia. x 1½ in. long, has ⅜-in.-dia. x ⅝-in.-long turned tenon.

Drawer side, ½ in. x 4½ in. x 15¾ in.

Drawer bottom is let into grooves all around.

Sides of drawer are narrower than the two drawer fronts by the thickness of the drawer runner.

pulls, turned with integral tenons, are affixed to the two fronts with wedges from the inside. The drawer can be opened from either end. This push-me/pull-you orientation may be unique to Shaker furniture. Regardless, it makes the stand more interesting and useful.

ROBERT TREANOR, a former teacher in the woodworking program at San Francisco State University, builds and writes about furniture in the Bay area.

Corner Cupboard

BY GARRETT HACK

On every trip to the Shelburne Museum near Burlington, Vermont, I visit a favorite object—a small hanging corner cabinet. With a single curved door, nicely shaped cornice, and molded base, the cabinet beams from its corner. Shelburne's cabinet was on my mind as I set about designing one for my house. The result is a country-style piece with delicate details. But you can change the moldings or details to transform the basic design to anything from Shaker to Craftsman.

Because so much of the carcase is hidden, a possibility is to build most of it from a less-expensive secondary wood and the facade from some special figured wood. Many old corner cabinets have the interior or just the shelves painted, which always adds an element of surprise and delight upon opening the door. I decided on butternut, walnut's country cousin, for the entire piece because of its warm brown color, pleasing grain, and delightful workability with plane and chisel.

OCCUPYING LITTLE SPACE, this piece will enhance any room.

A Small Hanging Corner Cabinet

Mill the sides, the back, the two shelves, and the door panels at the same time, as they are all the same ½-in. thickness. The shelves will later be planed to fit snugly in the ⁷⁄₁₆-in. dadoes. Then mill the door stiles and rails, the door frame, the wings, and the top and bottom to their ¾-in. thickness.

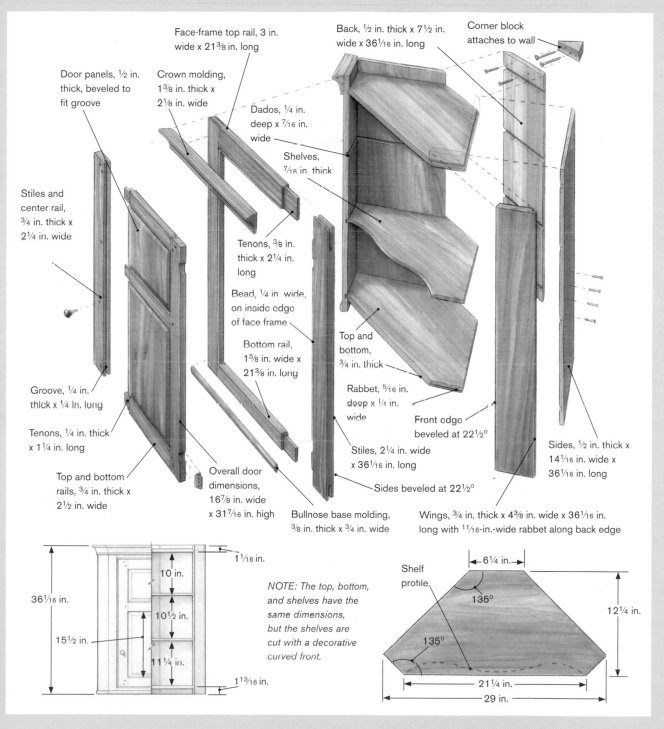

Face-frame top rail, 3 in. wide x 21³⁄₈ in. long

Back, ½ in. thick x 7½ in. wide x 36¹⁄₁₆ in. long

Corner block attaches to wall

Door panels, ½ in. thick, beveled to fit groove

Crown molding, 1³⁄₈ in. thick x 2¹⁄₈ in. wide

Dados, ¼ in. deep x ⁷⁄₁₆ in. wide

Shelves, ⁷⁄₁₆ in. thick

Stiles and center rail, ¾ in. thick x 2¼ in. wide

Tenons, ³⁄₈ in. thick x 2¼ in. long

Bead, ¼ in. wide, on inside edge of face frame

Bottom rail, 1⁵⁄₈ in. wide x 21³⁄₈ in. long

Top and bottom, ¾ in. thick

Rabbet, ⁵⁄₁₆ in. deep x ¼ in. wide

Groove, ¼ in. thick x ¼ in. long

Tenons, ¼ in. thick x 1¼ in. long

Top and bottom rails, ¾ in. thick x 2½ in. wide

Overall door dimensions, 16⁷⁄₈ in. wide x 31⁷⁄₁₆ in. high

Stiles, 2¼ in. wide x 36¹⁄₁₆ in. long

Sides beveled at 22½°

Front edge beveled at 22½°

Sides, ½ in. thick x 14¹⁄₁₆ in. wide x 36¹⁄₁₆ in. long

Bullnose base molding, ³⁄₈ in. thick x ¾ in. wide

Wings, ¾ in. thick x 4³⁄₈ in. wide x 36¹⁄₁₆ in. long with ¹¹⁄₁₆-in.-wide rabbet along back edge

1¹⁄₁₆ in.

36¹⁄₁₆ in.

10 in.

15½ in.

10½ in.

11¼ in.

1¹³⁄₁₆ in.

NOTE: The top, bottom, and shelves have the same dimensions, but the shelves are cut with a decorative curved front.

Shelf profile

6¼ in.

135°

135°

12¼ in.

21¼ in.

29 in.

Construct the Case Around the Shelves

LAY OUT THE PIECES. Use a combination gauge to lay out the lines on the top, bottom, and shelves where the wings will meet the sides.

PROFILE THE SHELVES. Stick the two shelves together with double-faced tape and then use the bandsaw to cut the profile on both front edges simultaneously.

JOIN THE WINGS AND SIDES. Check that the wings and sides meet at 90°, then glue and reinforce the joint with brads.

DRY-FIT THE CARCASE BEFORE FINAL ASSEMBLY. To check how the parts fit, lay one side and wing on the bench, insert the top, bottom, and shelves in their dadoes, then lower the other side into place (right). For the final assembly, secure the sides with glue and screws. Angle the holes forward so that the screws securing the top, bottom, and shelves bite into the grain. Attach the back using only screws to allow for movement (below).

Use a Full-Size Plan to Help Cut Parts With Odd Angles

Drawing out a full-size plan helps me visualize the relation of the parts, their angles, and the way they join together. It also allows me to lift dimensions and joinery details directly from the drawing, which results in fewer errors.

Mill the sides, the back, the two shelves, and the door panels at the same time, as they are all the same ½-in. thickness. The most economical and efficient way to do this is to resaw an 8/4 plank, grain-match the pieces, and glue up the parts. If you had some wide boards, so much the better. Then mill the door stiles and rails, the door frame, the wings, and the top and bottom to their ¾-in. thickness. Leave every part square edged for now. Make some extra pieces of both thicknesses for trial setups when cutting the joinery.

Cut to length the sides, wings, and back, and lay out the four dado cuts on one of the parts. This would be the time to customize the number of shelves and the height between them. I cut the dadoes with the tablesaw and dado set, although you could just as easily use a router. Reference each cut from the bottom of each part, and run the same dado on the back, wings, and sides with each setup. The dadoes are ⁷⁄₁₆ in. wide by ¼ in. deep; the shelves are planed to a snug fit. Be sure to run the same dado on a scrap or two to aid fitting the top and bottom later.

On each of the wings, first rabbet one edge, at least ³⁄₁₆ in. wider than the thickness of the sides to create a small extension for fitting the cabinet to the wall later. Referencing from the rabbeted side, cut each wing to width and at the bevel angle it will meet the door frame—22½°. Plane this edge straight and clean for a tight-fitting miter. Cut the cabinet sides to width and

their back edges at 45°. Plane and sand the insides of the sides and the wings and glue them together. Make sure the dadoes are perfectly aligned and the parts are square to one another. Clamp them and add a few small screws or brads.

Next, cut the shelves, top, and bottom to shape, measuring from the plan. A useful way to get all of these parts the same size is to clamp them together and plane each set of four edges at once. Check with a large square that the two sides are angled at 90°.

The top and bottom are rabbeted on all edges but the front, to produce a tongue to be fitted into the dadoes in the back, sides, and wings. When making the rabbet on the bottom of the top, note that it's a visible surface. Finish-plane the inside surface of the bottom (the first shelf) before creating the tongue, so as not to change its size. Make some trial cuts on scrap to produce a tongue slightly oversize and just shy of bottoming out in its dado. I fitted each tongue with a rabbet plane to a snug fit to a dado cut in scrap (so as not to damage the actual piece). Chamfer the edges of the tongue so that it will enter the dado easily when gluing up.

Dry-Fit the Case and Shape the Shelves

Dry-fit the two side and wing pieces, the shelves, and the top and bottom, using a screw or two to hold things together, if needed. Now mark where the curve of the shelves starts, on the inside of the cabinet where the bevel of the wing and door frame meets. The fronts of the top, bottom, and shelves should be flush with the inside edge of the wings' bevel. The backs of the top, bottom, and shelves should extend nearly ¼ in. to enter the dadoes in the back piece.

Build and Fit the Face Frame to the Cupboard

BEAD THE INSIDE EDGE. The inside edges of the stiles and rails each get a bead. This can be cut using a scratch stock, a router, or a molding plane.

CUT THE BRIDLE JOINT. Use a tenon jig to cut a slot in the end of each stile of the face frame. Cut a matching tenon to complete the bridle joint. The rails of the face frame are tenoned to fit the slot in the stiles.

A NEATER JOINT. To allow the bead to be mitered, cut away a strip of the tenon that matches the width of the bead. Miter the beads. Using a guide block that straddles the sections of face frame, miter the beading at a 45° angle with a chisel.

THE FINISHED BRIDLE JOINT. The mitered beading gives a nice surround to the door. Once the frame has been glued up, sand the miter joint smooth.

FIT THE FACE FRAME. Check that the wings and face frame form a tight miter joint, and that the frame contacts the top and bottom of the cabinet.

BEVEL THE FACE FRAME. Rip a 22½° bevel on the stiles of the face frame. Make sure to leave a little margin that can be planed away when fitting the frame.

A TRICKY CLAMPING ANGLE. Clamp a strip of wood with one corner beveled at 22½° to the face frame. Use this as a caul to draw the face frame and the wing together at the correct angle.

Attach the Crown Molding

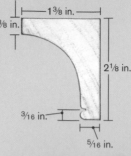

— 1⅜ in. —

⅜ in.

2⅛ in.

3/16 in.

5/16 in.

A PERFECT FIT. When mitering the molding, fit the center section first, and then cut the side sections to fit.

A HIDDEN NAIL HOLDS THE MOLDING. Use the quirk between the bead and the cove to hide the brads that help secure the crown molding to the face frame. Trim to fit. The molding and the wings extend past the sides of the cabinet by 3/16 in. to allow the cabinet to be trimmed to fit the wall.

Disassemble the case and mark out the shape of the front edge of the shelves. Cut close to the line on the bandsaw and spokeshave it to a smooth and fair curve. If you wish to display plates, cut a plate groove in the shelves and/or bottom with the tablesaw or router. The groove should be ¼ in. deep by ⅜ in. wide, and 2¼ in. away from the sides.

Bead and Build the Door Frame

The door frame consists of two rails and two stiles. The frame strengthens the cabinet, adds rigidity to the door opening, and provides a place to attach the cornice and base moldings. The stiles of the frame have beveled edges that mate with the cabinet's wings. Leave the stiles at least 5/16 in. oversize in width and square edged.

Before cutting any joints, bead the inside edges of the stiles and rails with a scratch stock, a router, or a molding plane. Use scrap wood to set up the tablesaw to cut the slots and tenons for bridle joints that connect the rails and stiles. To produce the neat appearance of a mitered bead at each inside corner of the door frame, cut away a section of wood from the side of the tenon and the slot. The width of this cut is equal to the width of the bead. With a guide block straddling the stiles and rails, use a chisel to pare away the bead and quirk at a 45° angle.

Trial-fit the door frame and beads, sand the beads smooth, and mark out and cut mortises for the hinges. Finally, glue the frame together, leaving it oversize in width.

Assemble the Case and Attach the Face Frame

Before assembling the case, plane or sand the shelves and inside surfaces of the top (the bottom was done earlier). Do one last dry-fit of the entire case, less the door frame and back, which are added later. Drill holes in the sides for the screws, angling them toward the front to grab some of the side grain of the top, bottom, and shelves.

Glue in the bottom, shelves, and top to one side, then, with this assembly on its side, add the other side. Very little glue is needed.

Be careful not to damage the exposed miters on the wings. Check that the shelves, top, and bottom are in their proper position, and screw the case together. Cut the back to size, plane or sand the inside surface, and attach it to the sides using screws but no glue because it is cross-grain to the shelves.

The last and trickiest part of the assembly is to fit the door frame. To gauge the location of the miters, stand the frame on the top of the cabinet centered in the opening, with the back surface of the frame against the front edge of the top. Mark the miters with a pencil, and then go to the

Details Can Define a Style

Changing the style of the case moldings and panels can dramatically change the appearance of this cabinet. For instance, the Shaker-style corner cupboard could have moldings of bullnose, and the Craftsman-style one could be built with flat panels and large, flat angled cornice molding.

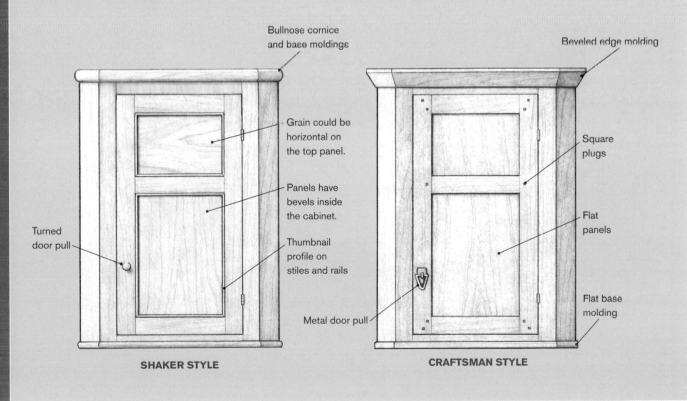

Bullnose cornice and base moldings

Grain could be horizontal on the top panel.

Panels have bevels inside the cabinet.

Thumbnail profile on stiles and rails

Turned door pull

SHAKER STYLE

Beveled edge molding

Square plugs

Flat panels

Flat base molding

Metal door pull

CRAFTSMAN STYLE

Build and Hang a Frame-and-Panel Door

RAISED DOOR PANELS. The delicate bevel on the front of the door panels can be cut with handplanes. A block plane works best on the end-grain bevels.

ASSEMBLE THE DOOR. The cabinet door is a frame-and-panel design with mortise-and-tenon joinery. The horns on the ends of the stiles are sawn away after the door has been glued.

MARK THE HINGE LOCATIONS. With the door held in place, transfer the hinge locations from the face frame to the door.

CHOP THE MORTISES. When cutting the hinge mortises in one of the stiles, protect the door from the clamp with a piece of leather or other padding.

tablesaw and rip both at 22½°, leaving the lines.

What's tricky about the final fitting is maintaining the miter angles where the frame and wings mate, and fitting the frame tightly against the top and bottom. With a handplane, take a shaving at a time from the frame and/or the top of the wings, checking both of these fits.

Both long-edge miters are glued as well as the front edges of the top and bottom. Apply glue sparingly so as to not have much squeeze out on the inside surfaces, where it will be difficult to clean up. To achieve clamping pressure at the correct angle for the miter joint, rip a 22½° bevel on one corner of two strips of scrap wood. Clamp a strip to each stile and then use clamps pulling on the strip and the back of the case to pull the miter together (see the bottom right photo on p. 127).

Moldings Wrap Around the Top and Bottom

Changing the style of the case moldings can dramatically change the appearance of this cabinet. The Shakers would have used the barest bullnose for the cornice and base, while the Pennsylvania Dutch favored far bolder and more detailed moldings. I chose a cove for the crown that can be cut on the tablesaw or a shaper, with a scratched bead at the base. The bullnose base molding is formed on a router table.

Starting with the center section, mark and miter the molding around the front of the cabinet. Each piece can be glued in place and secured with brads from the front or with small screws from behind. The side pieces should extend right to the outside edge of the wings so that they can be fitted to the wall with a block plane when the cabinet is hung.

Build and Hang the Door

When building the frame-and-panel door, size the stiles and rails ever so slightly large to allow some planing for a final fit. Lay out and cut the mortise and tenons. Cut grooves for the panels all relative to the front face of the door.

The panels can be made many ways: a traditional fielded panel, a flat panel, a panel with beaded edges, or one with very fine bevels, as in this design. After dry-fitting the door and panels, disassemble the cupboard enough to remove the panels, and chamfer the inside edges of the frame with a plane.

Plane and sand the door parts, then glue them together. Fit the door tightly to its opening by first fitting along the hinge side, then the bottom edge, the other stile edge, and the top edge. The final fitting happens after the door has been hung. Secure the hinges to the door frame (in their previously cut mortises), hold the door in place against them, mark out the hinge locations, and cut the mortises on the door stile. Hang the door and adjust the final fit by planing the unhinged stile and top or bottom rail. The last step in building the cabinet is to turn a knob and wedge it in place.

Apply a Finish and Hang the Cabinet

I finished this cabinet with three coats of a thinned oil/varnish mixture, and buffed out the final coat with 0000 steel wool and my special beeswax finish.

The simplest way to hang the cabinet is to find the first two wall studs away from the corner and screw into them through the sides above the top. Place a third screw through the top of the back into a corner block secured to the wall. Fit the cabinet to the wall by planing the small extensions at the sides.

GARRETT HACK is a contributing editor to *Fine Woodworking* magazine.

Step-Back Cupboard

BY MIKE DUNBAR

My wife had a narrow space in the kitchen where she wanted more storage. She had pestered me to make a piece of furniture to solve her problem, but I always had other things to do. One day I came home to discover she had bought a factory-made cupboard at a furniture store to fill the spot. One of the major reasons why I am a woodworker is that I want to be surrounded by furniture that is better than the mass-produced stuff. Factory furniture offends all of my sensibilities: It often lacks individuality, character, and craftsmanship; its designs are limited by the capabilities of machinery; and every surface is sanded to death.

I promised my wife that if she returned the piece, I would make something that we both liked better. She selected an antique cupboard on which this one is based. Besides the additional storage, she was happy to gain display space for some of her favorite items. The cupboard's small size also makes the piece versatile, and it can be used in any room if she redecorates or if we move.

BUILD THIS ELEGANT 18TH-CENTURY CUPBOARD and hone your hand-tool skills at the same time.

Painted Pine Cupboard

The 18th-century cupboard is made of ¾-in.-thick white pine and finished with milk paint.

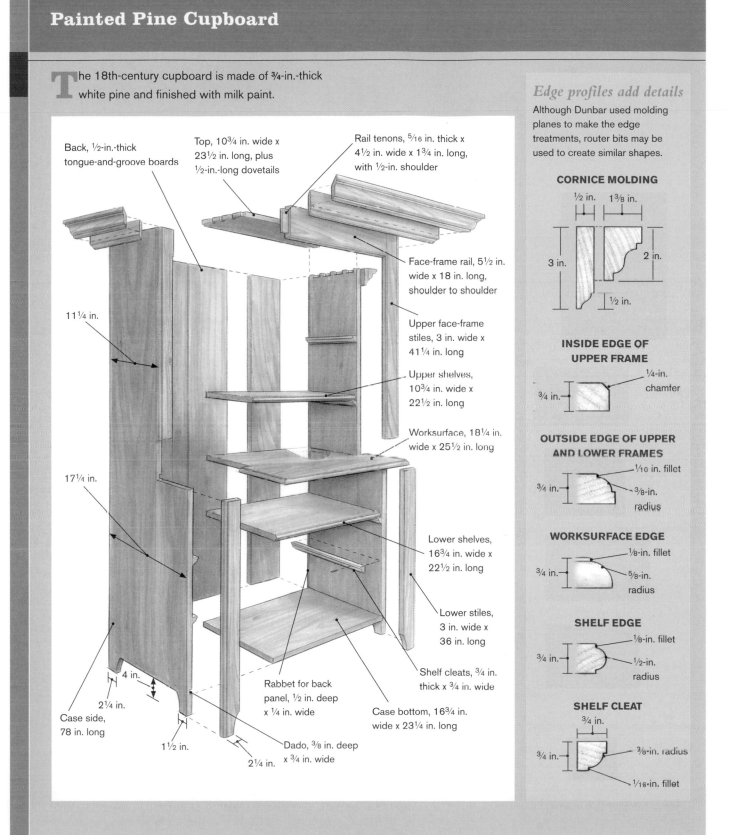

Back, ½-in.-thick tongue-and-groove boards

Top, 10¾ in. wide x 23½ in. long, plus ½-in.-long dovetails

Rail tenons, 5/16 in. thick x 4½ in. wide x 1¾ in. long, with ½-in. shoulder

11¼ in.

Face-frame rail, 5½ in. wide x 18 in. long, shoulder to shoulder

Upper face-frame stiles, 3 in. wide x 41¼ in. long

Upper shelves, 10¾ in. wide x 22½ in. long

17¼ in.

Worksurface, 18¼ in. wide x 25½ in. long

Lower shelves, 16¾ in. wide x 22½ in. long

Lower stiles, 3 in. wide x 36 in. long

4 in.

2¼ in.

Case side, 78 in. long

1½ in.

2¼ in.

Rabbet for back panel, ½ in. deep x ¼ in. wide

Dado, 3/8 in. deep x ¾ in. wide

Shelf cleats, ¾ in. thick x ¾ in. wide

Case bottom, 16¾ in. wide x 23¼ in. long

Edge profiles add details

Although Dunbar used molding planes to make the edge treatments, router bits may be used to create similar shapes.

CORNICE MOLDING

½ in.   1 3/8 in.

3 in.   2 in.

½ in.

INSIDE EDGE OF UPPER FRAME

¼-in. chamfer

¾ in.

OUTSIDE EDGE OF UPPER AND LOWER FRAMES

1/10 in. fillet

¾ in.   3/8-in. radius

WORKSURFACE EDGE

1/8-in. fillet

¾ in.   5/8-in. radius

SHELF EDGE

1/8-in. fillet

¾ in.   ½-in. radius

SHELF CLEAT

¾ in.

¾ in.   3/8-in. radius

1/16-in. fillet

The original piece that inspired this project was made in the late 18th century. The wood used in the original—eastern white pine—suggests that the piece was made in New England. While very handsome, the cupboard is not particularly complicated, especially if it is made using machines. However, the project presents a good opportunity to hone hand skills. So, even if you do use machines for most of the steps, I urge you to try at least some of the steps by hand.

Cut Stock to Rough Dimensions

I purchased 4/4 stock that I dimensioned with a jointer and a thickness planer. This is an important step because the stock must be perfectly flat. If I buy wood that already has been planed to thickness, I have to work with whatever warp or wind it has experienced while it was in the dealer's rack.

Begin by laying out the various parts on the lumber. Select the straightest and best lengths for the sides and the frame-and-panel door. You don't want any warp or twist in these most visible sections of the cabinet.

Cut out the various parts to oversize dimensions. You will cut them to their final dimensions later. Finally, joint one surface of each board and plane them all to thickness. Use a handplane on each part to remove the planer marks as well as any dings or scratches that have occurred along the way.

Cut and Assemble the Carcase Pieces

Cut the pieces for the carcase to their final dimensions. Each side of the cupboard has a long piece running the full height of the cupboard and a shorter piece that completes the bottom portion. When glued together, they create the step-back profile. These short joints are a nice place to practice jointing with a plane. Clamp the two boards face to face and plane them at the same time. This ensures they mate well. Unless you have stock wide enough to be used for the door panel as well as the work-surface, you also will need to joint and glue up these pieces.

Dadoes in the sides hold the bottom board and the work surface. The dadoes can be completed fairly easily with machine tools, but I chose to use a dado plane. For a couple of dadoes, this tool is just as fast and a lot more fun than a table-saw or router. Dado planes are not hard to find and can be purchased from used hand-tool dealers. They feature two nickers (cutters) that scribe the wood and help the tool cut across the grain. To ensure that the

Carcase Dimensions

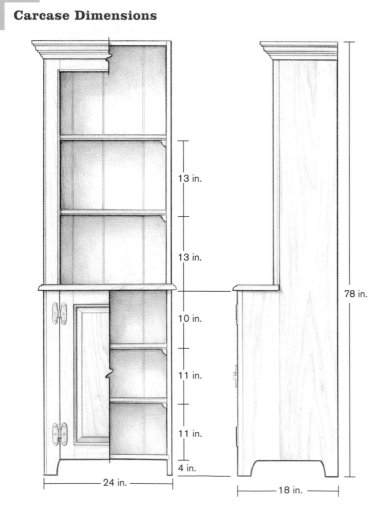

13 in.

13 in.

10 in.

11 in.

11 in.

4 in.

24 in.

78 in.

18 in.

Construct the Carcase

FORM THE STEP-BACK PRO-FILE. The base is built up by adding a short board to each case side.

JOINT THE EDGES. By clamping the face of the short board to the face of the case where they meet, both boards may be planed simultaneously, ensuring that they will meet up perfectly.

GLUE AND CLAMP THE TWO BOARDS. The show side can be handplaned to clean up any tool marks or excess glue.

ASSEMBLE THE CARCASE. The first step is to glue and clamp the case bottom to the cupboard sides.

JOIN THE DOVETAILS WITH GENTLE FORCE. With the bottom securely in place, apply glue to the dovetails and tap the top board into place.

CLAMPING THE TOP TO THE SIDES. Clamp blocks, positioned with wooden hand screws, provide gripping surfaces for the clamps to pull the dovetail joint tight.

SLIDE THE WORKSURFACE INTO THE DADOES. The cupboard worksurface should fit tightly in the dadoes cut into the cupboard sides. It is secured in place with glue and nails. The dadoes are hidden by the front of the worksurface.

dadoes line up perfectly, butt together the two side boards and pass the dado plane across both boards. It will take several passes to cut the upper and lower dadoes to their depth.

Cut rabbets along the back edge of the carcase to accept the back boards. This step would be faster if done with machine tools, but I did the job with a rabbet plane, which is adjustable for width and depth.

Next, lay out and cut the dovetails that join the top board to the side panels. I chose to use half-blind dovetails. They require a bit more work, but they make the project more interesting. Finally, trace the foot pattern on the bottom of both side boards using a template and cut out the feet with a coping saw. You might find it easiest to cut the curved portion with your coping saw and then use a panel saw to finish off the straight cut. The rough spots can be cleaned up with a spokeshave or rasp.

The carcase is assembled by first gluing and nailing the case bottom into the cup-

board sides. Next, assemble the top to the cupboard sides. Clamp the dovetails while the glue sets.

When nails are exposed, as is the case with this project, I prefer to use cut nails. Their long, narrow heads are less obvious than the round heads of drawn finish nails. The right nails for this work are 6d fine finish cut nails.

After the carcase has been glued up, tack a cross brace across the back to keep it square while you work on it for the remaining steps.

Mold and Attach the Face Frames

The upper face frame is made up of three pieces. I laid out the mortise-and-tenon joints with a marking gauge and cut the tenons with a backsaw, and the mortises with a mortise chisel. When done, test-fit the face frame to the carcase. If necessary, plane the outside edges flush.

Edge the upper face frame The inside edges of the frame are chamfered, which can be done with a chamfering plane if you have one. The chamfers on this frame are so narrow that you can lay them out with a marking gauge and cut them with a block plane. The chamfers on the stiles are stopped, and the plane will not reach into the corners, so complete the chamfers at the corners with a drawknife. A drawknife typically is used for coarse work, but with a steady hand, the tool can take fine shavings. Use a sharp chisel to complete the mitered corners where the chamfers meet.

Cut the ovolo profile on the outside of the stiles. This is an important detail. Although small, this profile softens the cupboard's vertical corners while giving them definition. Used above and below, the ovolo also ties together the open top and closed bottom.

Because I had to nail through the molding profile to attach the stiles to the carcase,

Add the Face Frames and Cornice

THE UPPER FACE FRAME GETS A CHAMFER ON ITS INSIDE EDGE. Scribe the width with a marking gauge and use a block plane to bevel the inside edge of the top rail.

ATTACH THE FACE FRAME. Once the upper face frame has been assembled, glue and nail it onto the cupboard.

THE UPPER FACE-FRAME STILES REQUIRE A STOPPED CHAMFER. Dry-fit the frame and mark the end of the chamfer (left), then plane the chamfer to within an inch or two of the stop mark. A drawknife will give you a smooth edge (center) as you cut away the remainder of the chamfer. Dry-fit again and finish the corner with a chisel (right).

I used 4d headless cut brads (1½ in.), which are less visible than the larger 6d cut nails.

Thumbnail Edge Completes the Worksurface

The worksurface separates the open top section of the cupboard from the lower, enclosed portion. Before cutting and fitting the worksurface into the cupboard, add a thumbnail profile to its exposed edges. The thumbnail profile was common on 18th-century furniture. I made mine with a molding plane. Cut the molding on the end grain first. A waste strip on the far corner keeps the wood from chipping out on the exposed front corners. Now cut the thumbnail on the front, in the direction of the grain.

Attach the lower face-frame stiles

The lower face frame has only two stiles and no rails. Like the stiles on the upper face frame, the outside edges of the lower stiles are molded with an ovolo profile. Before securing the stiles to the carcase, cut out the feet to the same pattern as the sides. To protect the molding, I again used headless brads, but I used 6d nails to secure the stiles to the bottom board. A nail through the worksurface also strengthens the stile-to-case connection. I don't use any glue.

Locate and Cut the Shelf Cleats

The placement of the shelves is determined by what you plan to put in each section of the cupboard. The shelves are held in place within the cupboard by cleats.

Because some of the cleats in the open portion of the cupboard are visible, they are decorated with the same ovolo profile as the face-frame stiles. The easiest way to make these cleats is to cut the molding on the edge of a board. Rip off a strip to the width given in the drawing, and then cut the cleats to length. If you do not have stock long enough for all 10 cleats, run multiple strips.

Cut the cleats to length and nail them into the cupboard's upper and lower sections. Because the carcase sides are only ¾ in. thick and don't provide a lot of material for nailing, I also added a spot of glue in the middle of each cleat. The cleats run across the sides, but the nails are forgiving enough to accommodate seasonal movement. Also, gluing only in the center allows movement. The shelves are not secured to the cleats; gravity holds them in place.

Make an edge on the shelves The molding profile on the front edges of the shelves is called an astragal and was a common 18th-century treatment for shelves. Its similarity to the ovolos on the carcase and

ADD A CORNICE TO THE TOP. The cornice, shaped with a molding plane, is built up from two layers to achieve its pronounced profile.

SECURE THE LOWER STILES TO THE CASE. Use 4d headless cut brads through the molding into the sides and 6d cut nails into the bottom.

Hand-Cut Frame-and-Panel Door

Raise the door panel with a molding plane. Wedges, not glue, secure the tenons in the mortises.

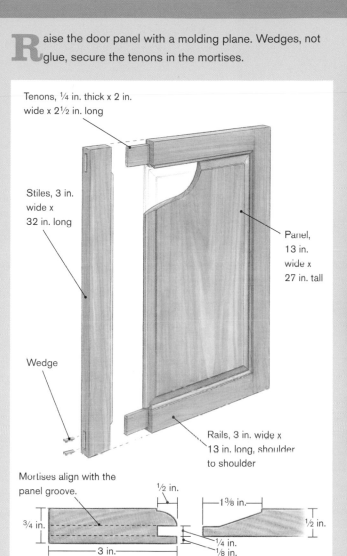

Tenons, ¼ in. thick x 2 in. wide x 2½ in. long

Stiles, 3 in. wide x 32 in. long

Wedge

Panel, 13 in. wide x 27 in. tall

Rails, 3 in. wide x 13 in. long, shoulder to shoulder

Mortises align with the panel groove.

½ in.
1⅜ in.
¾ in.
3 in.
¼ in.
⅛ in.
½ in.

MITER THE THUMBNAIL MOLDING

MITER THE INSIDE CORNERS OF THE DOOR FRAME. Saw and chisel away the waste. Cut the stiles slightly longer than the finished door to add strength to the board when chopping the mortises. The extra length, known as a horn, can be trimmed away once the door is assembled.

A JIG FOR PERFECT MITERS. When cutting the miters on the door stiles and rails, use a jig with a 45° slope to guide your chisel.

ASSEMBLE THE DOOR AND WEDGE THE TENONS. Drive wedges into the tenons to secure them tightly in the offset mortises. Typical 18th-century tenoned doors were left unglued. Pinning the tenons will add even more strength.

the thumbnail on the worksurface help tie together the piece's design.

You also can cut a groove in each shelf with a shoulder plane to prop up plates for display. Clamp a straightedge to the shelf and use this as a fence to guide the shoulder plane. Holding the plane at an angle will cut the V-shaped groove.

Complete the Carcase with a Cornice

Because this cupboard is so narrow and tall, it needs to be balanced with a large cornice. As long as you design the cornice to the prescribed dimensions, it does not matter what profile you use. I own a nice profile called a stepped reverse ogee (cyma recta), but by itself it is not quite large enough for the piece. Therefore, I made a larger cornice by stacking two layers. The first layer has a small ogee (cyma reversa) that projects below the larger, resulting in a cornice with the necessary scale.

Nail on the Tongue-and-Groove Back Boards

In 18th-century furniture, it was common to see back boards of random widths. Cabinetmakers typically used the widest boards on hand and the fewest needed to fill the space. To achieve this feel, I used two wider boards on the sides and a narrow one in the middle. For these I used ½-in.-thick pine.

To avoid gaps in the back boards caused by seasonal movement, I cut tongues and grooves into their edges. I have a pair of planes that make this joint, called match planes. Like most hand tools, they are quick and easy for a small job like this.

The back boards are nailed into the rabbets in the cupboard sides. They also are nailed into the top and bottom boards and the worksurface. Once again, pay attention to seasonal movement. In the winter, fit the back boards loosely. In the summer, you should snug them up, as they will shrink in the winter.

Make the Door Parts by Hand

The door is the most complicated piece of joinery in the cupboard. Using a plow plane, the first task is to cut a groove in the inside edge of each door stile. Next, cut a molding on the outer edge with the same plane used to make the thumbnail on the worksurface. It is easiest to cut these profiles on long stock and then crosscut the stiles and rails from these strips.

Make the stiles slightly longer than the finished door. That way, you have extra length to help prevent the stiles from splitting when you're chopping the mortises. This extra length, known as a horn, can be trimmed after the door has been assembled.

Before cutting the mortise-and-tenons, identify all of the surfaces on the stiles and rails that will be facing out. The mortises are slightly offset and do not pass through the center of the stile's thickness. This will require laying out the mortises with the identical placement on both edges. And be sure to place the fence of the mortise gauge on the same surface of the stiles and rails. By always marking pieces with identifiers you will be able to cut consistently. The mortises are cut through, which means you can see the ends of the tenons in the edges of the stiles.

To avoid blowing out the back side of the stile when making the mortises, cut from both sides and then meet in the middle. You will have to trim away the thumbnail to join the mortise and tenons.

Raise the door panel I have a very nice panel-raising plane that I enjoy using, so I made the panel by hand. When making only one panel, the plane is about as fast as the tablesaw or router, which also will make this cut. Measure the panel's length and width from the bottom of the grooves in the stiles and rails. If you live in an area of the country with cold winters and humid summers, accommodate the panel's seasonal shrinkage and expansion across its grain by adjusting the width accordingly. If you are making the cupboard in the summer, you should create a snug fit. If you're making it in winter, fit the panel loosely, as it will swell in the humid summer.

After testing the panel's fit, complete the door assembly. In the 18th century, doors usually were not glued, and over the centuries these doors have not sagged, so I followed suit and did not use any glue. Two wedges are driven into the ends of each tenon to tighten it in its mortise. You can strengthen the joint further by pinning the tenons.

After trimming the horns, plane the door's stiles to fit the opening. Your door's fit also will depend on the season. If you make a snug door in the winter, it will bind in the summer.

Finish With Fine Hardware and Milk Paint

The original cupboard's door was mounted with wrought-iron hinges and held shut with a wooden turn button. I spruced up mine with cast brass ornamental H-hinges and a matching catch. These items cost about $80*, but after all the work I put into the piece and the cost of the lumber, it seems only fitting.

Once the piece was complete, I finished it with milk paint. To match the color scheme of our home, I finished the outside surfaces of the cupboard with barn red. For the exposed inside walls and back boards, I used mustard.

Please note price estimates are from 2003.

MIKE DUNBAR is a contributing editor to *Fine Woodworking* magazine.

Sources

MOLDING PLANES
Tod Herrli
765-664-3325

HARDWARE
Horton Brasses
49 Nooks Hill Rd.
Cromwell, CT 06416
800-754-9127
www.horton-brasses.com

Ball and Ball
463 W. Lincoln Hwy.
Exton, PA 19341
800-257-3711
www.ballandball-us.com

CUT NAILS
Tremont Nail
P.O. Box 111
Wareham, MA 02571
800-842-0560
www.tremontnail.com

Pegged Post-and-Beam Armoire Knocks Down

BY CHRIS GOCHNOUR

The trouble with most armoires is that if they're big enough to fit all your clothes—or electronic gear, board games, or books—they're too big to fit through the door. This was brought home to me forcefully on several occasions when I received distress calls from people who, knowing I was a furniture maker, thought I might have a trick for shrinking the armoire they just bought to get it through their doorway. I soon found myself amputating a foot here, prying off a glued-on crown molding there. When I decided to build an armoire myself, I

THREE SKINS, ONE SKELETON. The author's armoires in an array of styles all use a centuries-old cabinet structure originally borrowed from post-and-beam houses. The post-and-beam structure makes a cabinet that is strong and handsome and perfectly accommodates wood movement. If the major joints are pegged instead of glued, the cabinet can also be knocked down for transport or repair. In the photo on the facing page, the skeleton of a country French armoire in knotty alder stands dry-assembled with all its parts and panels leaning against it.

Got It Pegged

The mortise-and-tenon frame joints in the cabinet below are held fast with drawbore pegs instead of glue, allowing easy disassembly for transport or repair.

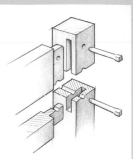

Drawbore pegs actually pull the tenon home. The hole through the tenon is offset slightly toward the shoulder so that when the peg is pounded in, the rail snugs up against the post.

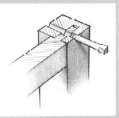

The shaft of the peg is waxed to make driving it easier. The square head bites in the round hole. To prevent splitting harder woods, square the hole with a chisel before driving in the peg.

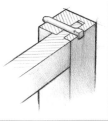

The peg extends through the post. Disassembling the joint requires just a few taps from inside with a hammer and a drift pin to knock out the peg.

NOTCH IT. After cutting the mortises for the rail tenons, the author uses a hollow-chisel mortiser to notch the posts where they accept the corners of the cabinet top and cabinet bottom.

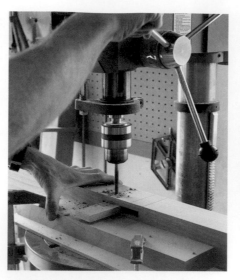

TEMPORARY TENON. A scrap the same thickness as the tenon fills the mortise to prevent tearout as the holes for the pegs are drilled.

DOUBLE DRILLING. Pairing up the posts makes it easy to cut the half-round notches for the shelf-support bars. It also ensures the notches will correspond exactly in height.

COLOR-CODED LAYOUT. Post layout is the most complex and crucial aspect of preparing to make a post-and-beam cabinet. To keep track of all the different parts that meet at the posts as well as the joints that secure them, the author uses a different colored pencil for each element.

discovered that a fine solution to this doorway dilemma has been around for centuries: the post-and-beam cabinet with pegged mortise-and-tenon joints.

Dutch and German *kasts*, Spanish *trasteros*, French *armoires,* and Chinese *gui* all were large storage cabinets designed around a straightforward post-and-beam structure, a system sturdy enough to have been employed as well to construct the very houses these cabinets resided in. Post-and-beam cabinet construction—vertical posts and horizontal beams connected by large mortise-and-tenon joints—creates a framework that, once secured with drawbore pegs, is very rigid and durable. Yet it can be easily disassembled into small, maneuverable components.

I particularly admire the beauty and grand scale of antique French armoires, and I've made several of them. But I've also built armoires in the Southwest style and the Arts-and-Crafts style, and I have found that the post-and-beam structure is adaptable to a range of styles.

Post-and-Beam Armoire

Main carcase joints are knockdown, secured with drawbore pegs.

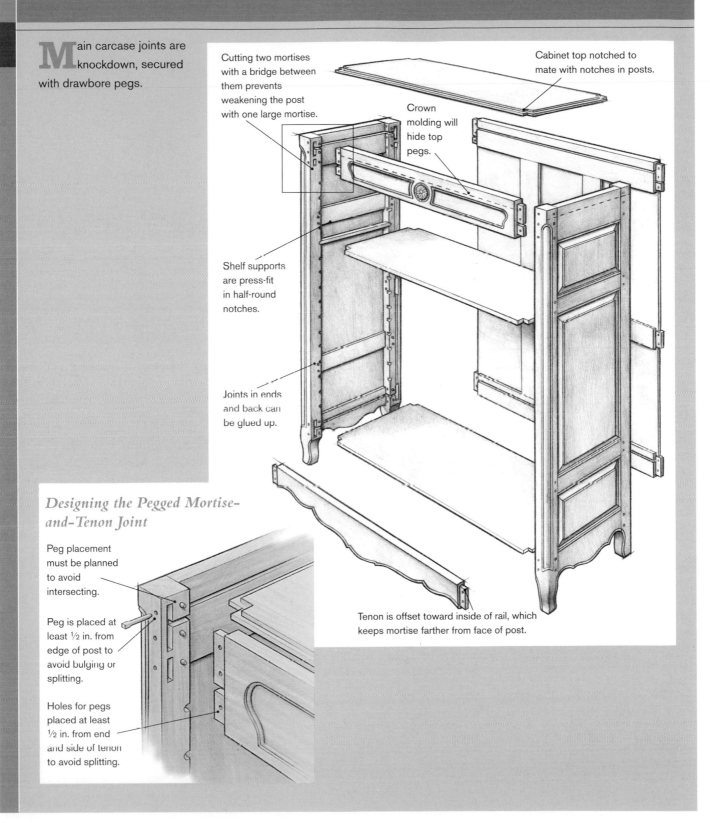

Cutting two mortises with a bridge between them prevents weakening the post with one large mortise.

Cabinet top notched to mate with notches in posts.

Crown molding will hide top pegs.

Shelf supports are press-fit in half-round notches.

Joints in ends and back can be glued up.

Tenon is offset toward inside of rail, which keeps mortise farther from face of post.

Designing the Pegged Mortise-and-Tenon Joint

Peg placement must be planned to avoid intersecting.

Peg is placed at least ½ in. from edge of post to avoid bulging or splitting.

Holes for pegs placed at least ½ in. from end and side of tenon to avoid splitting.

TWO-STEP GROOVE. The author cuts panel grooves with the frame assembled. To avoid tearout, he makes a shallow counterclockwise scoring cut before cutting full depth in a clockwise pass.

Inside-Out Design

Designing a post-and-beam cabinet begins with its primary skeletal structure: four corner posts connected by wide rails top and bottom. The strength of the cabinet is derived mainly from these members and the joinery that connects them. For maximum stability in my large country French armoire—90 in. high, 57½ in. wide, and 24 in. deep—I used posts a beefy 2⅝ in. sq. with rails ranging from 4 in. to 8 in. wide. Posts this big can accommodate large mortises without being unduly weakened; rails this wide have room for substantial shoulders along with wide tenons. On the widest rails, I used two tenons and left a bridge between them because a single large mortise would eliminate too much material and compromise the strength of the post.

After the basic skeleton is designed, I subdivide the cabinet sides and back using rails and muntins. The subdivision creates smaller, more manageable panel sizes, has a strong visual effect, and contributes to the overall strength of the cabinet.

Profile of a Peg

This cabinet uses a 3-in. peg for its 2⅝-in. posts. The pegs start out as ⁷⁄₁₆-in. square blanks. For this alder cabinet, the pegs are made of beech because it is a harder wood.

Top is left flat to accept hammer blows; its edges are broken by dragging across sandpaper.

Soft transition eases square head into round hole.

End is tapered to facilitate entry into offset hole in tenon.

PEGS' PARENTS. The author starts with long, square blanks and rounds a section at each end with a beading bit on the router table. He tapers the ends against a belt sander and then cuts the pegs to length on the tablesaw.

DON'T FORGET TO STEER WHEN YOU DRIVE. An adjustable crescent wrench keeps the head of the peg from twisting as it is driven home. The author leaves the peg one hammer tap proud of flush with the post.

Embellishing the framework is the final step in the design process. Because the primary skeletal structure doesn't differ much from piece to piece, it is largely the details that distinguish one post-and-beam cabinet from another. These can include decorative panels, doors, crown and other moldings, turnings, and carvings.

Layout Is the Linchpin

Laying out the joinery on the posts is the most complex and critical aspect of building a post-and-beam cabinet, because it is here that all of the components come together. On just one post there will be as many as eight mortises, 14 peg holes, two panel grooves, two notches for the top and bottom, and a dozen or more half-round notches for shelf supports. To make sense of this blizzard of joinery, I use a different colored pencil for each operation—one for mortises, another for peg holes, and so on. I lay out the joinery in this order:

- mortises for the rails
- notches for the cabinet top and cabinet bottom
- holes for the pegs
- rounded notches for adjustable shelf supports
- grooves for the panels

And then I set about machining all the joinery, following the same sequence.

Machining the Legs

I use a horizontal boring machine to cut the mortises and a benchtop hollow-chisel mortiser to square up the ends. But you can cut the mortises in several different ways as long as you lay them out properly, size them correctly, and mill them cleanly. I cut the tenons on the tablesaw with multiple passes over a dado head and adjust to a piston-fit with a shoulder plane.

Because the cabinet top and cabinet bottom float in a groove in the rails, I must make corresponding notches on the inside corners of the legs. I use a hollow-chisel mortiser to make these notches (see the top left photo on p. 144), but simply drilling a series of holes and then squaring them up with a chisel works fine.

After the peg locations have been laid out, I drill the holes for them on a drill press. I use a fence to ensure a consistent location of the holes on each leg. To eliminate tearout as the drill bit pierces the mortise, I fill the mortise with a scrap of wood the same thickness as the tenons (see the center photo at top on p. 144). I also use a sacrificial scrap below the post to avoid tearout when the bit exits the bottom face of the post.

I use a traditional type of adjustable shelving, one suited both to the style and the structure of post-and-beam cabinets. For shelf supports, it uses wooden bars, which are press-fit into rounded notches in

the posts. To make these notches, I clamp the front and back legs together, being careful that they are aligned at the ends. Then I drill a series of holes with a Forstner bit so that half of each hole is on the front leg and half is on the back (see the top right photo on p. 144). This produces perfectly corresponding half-round notches in the paired posts. When I build an armoire with drawers, I use the same notches to house side-mounted wooden drawer runners.

Clamp Up the Side Frame for More Machining

The next two steps are best accomplished with the cabinet's sides assembled, without panels. Later, I will disassemble the sides, assemble the back, and repeat these steps.

I groove the legs and rails for the panels they will hold and cut the grooves with a router. Using a slot cutter with a bearing wheel, I just run the router around the frame. The one drawback to routing the grooves this way is that you wind up with rounded corners, but a sharp chisel makes quick work of squaring them up.

With the frame still clamped snugly, I insert a brad-point drill bit into each peg hole and, with a twist of my fingers, mark the hole's centerpoint on the tenon. Then I disassemble the cabinet side and drill the peg holes through the tenons on the drill press. I don't drill right on the centerpoint marks, but 1/32 in. toward the tenon's shoul-

der. When the peg is driven through, this vital 1/32 in. offset draws the tenon home tight and keeps the joints from loosening over time. In a cabinet built of soft wood, I would make the offset a shade more than 1/32; in the hardest woods, a shade under.

The Humble Peg

Holding all this work together is a handful of little pegs. I always make them of hardwood, and whatever wood I choose, I make sure it is as hard or slightly harder than the wood the pegs will be driven into.

I make the pegs by first milling square blanks 2 or 3 ft. long. I round 2½ in. or so at either end of the stick using a beading bit on a router table. Because the center section of the blank remains square, I still get good registration against the router table and fence even after the ends are cylindrical. Next I taper both ends of each long stick by turning them against a belt sander. Finally, I cut a peg from each end of the stick, leaving a ½-in.-long square section at the head. I repeat the steps to make more pegs, continuing until the blanks are getting too short to hold safely.

When I'm finished, I wax the peg shafts and get to the fun part—driving them home.

CHRIS GOCHNOUR builds furniture in Salt Lake City, Utah.

Credits

The articles in this book appeared in the following issues of *Fine Woodworking*:

p. 4: Harvest Table by Christian Becksvoort, issue 159. Photos by Matthew Teague, courtesy *Fine Woodworking*, © The Taunton Press, Inc., except photo on p. 4 by Dennis Griggs, courtesy *Fine Woodworking*, © The Taunton Press, Inc.; Drawings by Bob La Pointe, courtesy *Fine Woodworking*, © The Taunton Press, Inc.

p. 10: Pembroke Table by Jefferson Kolle, issue 138. Photos by Michael Pekovich, courtesy *Fine Woodworking*, © The Taunton Press, Inc.; Drawings by Bob La Pointe, courtesy *Fine Woodworking*, © The Taunton Press, Inc.

p. 18: One-Drawer Lamp Stand by Mike Dunbar, issue 142. Photos by Michael Pekovich, courtesy *Fine Woodworking*, © The Taunton Press, Inc.; Drawings by Bob La Pointe, courtesy *Fine Woodworking*, © The Taunton Press, Inc.

p. 28: Tip-Top Table by Mario Rodriguez, issue 173. Photos by Matt Berger, courtesy *Fine Woodworking*, © The Taunton Press, Inc.; Drawings by Bob La Pointe, courtesy *Fine Woodworking*, © The Taunton Press, Inc.

p. 38: Drop-Leaf Breakfast Table by Robert Treanor, issue 104. Photos by Jonathan Binzen, courtesy *Fine Woodworking*, © The Taunton Press, Inc.; Drawing by Lee Hov, courtesy *Fine Woodworking*, © The Taunton Press, Inc.

p. 44: Construct a Classic Bed by Doug Mooberry and Steve Latta, issue 105. Photos by Alec Waters, courtesy *Fine Woodworking*, © The Taunton Press, Inc.; Drawings by Lee Hov, courtesy *Fine Woodworking*, © The Taunton Press, Inc.

p. 51: Making a Sheraton Bed by Philip C. Lowe, issue 113. Photos by Charley Robinson, courtesy *Fine Woodworking*, © The Taunton Press, Inc.; Drawing on p. 53 by Kathleen Rushton, courtesy *Fine Woodworking*, © The Taunton Press, Inc.; Drawing on p. 54 by Mike Wanke, courtesy *Fine Woodworking*, © The Taunton Press, Inc.

p. 56: Shaker-Style Clock by Philip C. Lowe, issue 101. Photo by Susan Kahn, courtesy *Fine Woodworking*, © The Taunton Press, Inc.; Drawings by Heather Lambert, courtesy *Fine Woodworking*, © The Taunton Press, Inc.

p. 61: Shaker Tall Clock by Robert Treanor, issue 122. Photos by Scott Gibson, courtesy *Fine Woodworking*, © The Taunton Press, Inc., except photo on p. 62 (right) by Kaz Tsuruta, courtesy *Fine Woodworking*, © The Taunton Press, Inc.; Drawings by Bob La Pointe, courtesy *Fine Woodworking*, © The Taunton Press, Inc.

p. 69: 18th-Century Six-Board Chest by Mike Dunbar, issue 134. Photos by Jefferson Kolle, courtesy *Fine Woodworking*, © The Taunton Press, Inc., except photo on p. 76 by Michael Pekovich, courtesy *Fine Woodworking*, © The Taunton Press, Inc.; Drawings by Tim Langenderfer, courtesy *Fine Woodworking*, © The Taunton Press, Inc.

p. 77: A Shaker Blanket Chest by Charles Durfee, issue 172. Photos by Mark Schofield, courtesy *Fine Woodworking*, © The Taunton Press, Inc., except photo on p. 77 by Michael Pekovich, courtesy *Fine Woodworking*, © The Taunton Press, Inc.; Drawings by Fred Carlson, courtesy *Fine Woodworking*, © The Taunton Press, Inc.

p. 87: Captain's Desk Is Compact and Efficient by Cameron Russell, issue 104. Photos by Trevor Mills, courtesy of Cameron Russell; Drawings by Bob La Pointe, courtesy *Fine Woodworking*, © The Taunton Press, Inc.

p. 93: Cherry Chest of Drawers by Michael Pekovich, issue 170. Photos by Matt Berger, courtesy *Fine Woodworking*, © The Taunton Press, Inc.; Drawings by Bob La Pointe, courtesy *Fine Woodworking*, © The Taunton Press, Inc.

p. 105: Building a Strong, Light Carcase by Garrett Hack, issue 104. Photos by Vincent Laurence, courtesy *Fine Woodworking*, © The Taunton Press, Inc., except photo on p. 105 by John Sheldon, courtesy *Fine Woodworking*, © The Taunton Press, Inc.; Drawings by Bob La Pointe, courtesy *Fine Woodworking*, © The Taunton Press, Inc.

p. 111: A Small Bureau Built to Last by Robert Treanor, issue 109. Photos by Jonathan Binzen, courtesy *Fine Woodworking*, © The Taunton Press, Inc.; Drawings by David Dann, courtesy *Fine Woodworking*, © The Taunton Press, Inc.

p. 117: Shaker Sewing Stand Remains Stylish, Practical by Robert Treanor, issue 116. Photos by Alec Waters, courtesy *Fine Woodworking*, © The Taunton Press, Inc. except photo on p. 117 by Kaz Tsuruta, courtesy *Fine Woodworking*, © The Taunton Press, Inc., photo on p. 119 (bottom) by Robert Treanor, courtesy *Fine Woodworking*, © The Taunton Press, Inc., and photo on p. 120 (bottom) by John Kassay, courtesy *Fine Woodworking*, © The Taunton Press, Inc.; Drawings by Bob La Pointe, courtesy *Fine Woodworking*, © The Taunton Press, Inc.

p. 122: Corner Cupboard by Garrett Hack, issue 175. Photos by Mark Schofield, courtesy *Fine Woodworking*, © The Taunton Press, Inc.

p. 132: Step-Back Cupboard by Mike Dunbar, issue 165. Photos by Matt Berger, courtesy *Fine Woodworking*, © The Taunton Press, Inc.; Drawings by Bob La Pointe, courtesy *Fine Woodworking*, © The Taunton Press, Inc.

p. 142: Pegged Post-and-Beam Armoire Knocks Down by Chris Gochnour, issue 132. Photos by Jonathan Binzen, courtesy *Fine Woodworking*, © The Taunton Press, Inc., except photo on p. 142 (center) by Rob Stout, courtesy *Fine Woodworking*, © The Taunton Press, Inc.; Drawings by Bob La Pointe, courtesy *Fine Woodworking*, © The Taunton Press, Inc.

Index

The New Best of Fine Woodworking series

A collection of the best articles from the last ten years of Fine Woodworking.

Designing Furniture
The New Best of Fine Woodworking
From the editors of FWW
ISBN 1-56158-684-6
Product #070767
$17.95 U.S.
$25.95 Canada

Small Woodworking Shops
The New Best of Fine Woodworking
From the editors of FWW
ISBN 1-56158-686-2
Product #070768
$17.95 U.S.
$25.95 Canada

Working with Routers
The New Best of Fine Woodworking
From the editors of FWW
ISBN 1-56158-685-4
Product #070769
$17.95 U.S.
$25.95 Canada

Building Small Projects
The New Best of Fine Woodworking
From the editors of FWW
ISBN 1-56158-730-3
Product #070791
$17.95 U.S.
$25.95 Canada

Designing and Building Cabinets
The New Best of Fine Woodworking
From the editors of FWW
ISBN 1-56158-732-X
Product #070792
$17.95 U.S.
$25.95 Canada

Traditional Finishing Techniques
The New Best of Fine Woodworking
From the editors of FWW
ISBN 1-56158-733-8
Product #070793
$17.95 U.S.
$25.95 Canada

Working with Tablesaws
The New Best of Fine Woodworking
From the editors of FWW
ISBN 1-56158-749-4
Product #070811
$17.95 U.S.
$25.95 Canada

Working with Handplanes
The New Best of Fine Woodworking
From the editors of FWW
ISBN 1-56158-748-6
Product #070810
$17.95 U.S.
$25.95 Canada

Workshop Machines
The New Best of Fine Woodworking
From the editors of FWW
ISBN 1-56158-765-6
Product #070826
$17.95 U.S.
$25.95 Canada

Selecting and Using Hand Tools
The New Best of Fine Woodworking
From the editors of FWW
ISBN 1-56158-783-4
Product #070810
$17.95 U.S.
$25.95 Canada

Workstations and Tool Storage
The New Best of Fine Woodworking
From the editors of FWW
ISBN 1-56158-785-0
Product #070838
$17.95 U.S.
$25.95 Canada

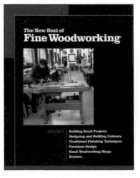

The New Best of Fine Woodworking Slipcase Set Volume 1

Designing Furniture
Working with Routers
Small Woodworking Shops
Designing and Building Cabinets
Building Small Projects
Traditional Finishing Techniques
The New Best of Fine Woodworking

From the editors of FWW
ISBN 1-56158-736-2
Product #070808
$85.00 U.S.
$120.00 Canada